BULL CITY SURVIVOR

Standing Up to a Hard Life in a Southern City

Simon Partner *and*
Emma Johnston

McFarland & Company, Inc., Publishers
Jefferson, North Carolina, and London

LIBRARY OF CONGRESS CATALOGUING-IN-PUBLICATION DATA

Partner, Simon, 1958–
    Bull city survivor : standing up to a hard life in a southern
city / Simon Partner and Emma Johnston.
        p.   cm.
    Includes bibliographical references and index.

    ISBN 978-0-7864-7447-9
    softcover : acid free paper ∞

    1. Johnston, Emma, 1950–   2. African Americans—
North Carolina—Durham—Social conditions—20th century.
3. African Americans—North Carolina—Durham—
Biography.   4. Segregation—North Carolina—Durham—
History.   5. Murder—North Carolina—Durham.
6. Durham (N.C.)—Social conditions—20th century.
7. Durham (N.C.)—Race relations—History—20th
century.   8. Durham (N.C.)—Biography.   I. Johnston,
Emma, 1950–   II. Title.
F264.D9P27 2013
975.6'563043092—dc23
[B]   2013024558

BRITISH LIBRARY CATALOGUING DATA ARE AVAILABLE

On the cover: *faces* liquidlibrary/Thinkstock
background iStockphoto/Thinkstock

Manufactured in the United States of America

McFarland & Company, Inc., Publishers
  Box 611, Jefferson, North Carolina 28640
  www.mcfarlandpub.com

To my Mama, to my husband
and our amazing family,
and also to my Lord Jesus Christ,
who is the savior of my soul.—Emma

To all those who work for peace and the resolution
of conflict, and particularly to the Durham Friends Meeting
and the Religious Coalition for a Nonviolent Durham.—Simon

BULL CITY
SURVIVOR

Table of Contents

Introduction
by Simon Partner

I first met Emma Johnston in October 2008. It had been a little over a year since the murder of her youngest child, Michael Lavaughan Johnston (both names are pseudonyms).

Michael was murdered in the parking lot of the Mangum Square apartment complex in August 2007. He was twenty-five years old. His murder was the twelfth so far that year in Durham, North Carolina, a city of 216,000 inhabitants. By the end of the year, another fourteen people would be killed. The majority of them were — like Michael — young African American men. Around half of the killings in Durham in recent years have been identified by the police as gang related.[1]

America is a violent country. It always has been. The gun is enshrined in our Constitution and emblazoned on our culture. But why do so many young people have to die every year in a city that in so many other ways represents the best in America? Durham is a fantastic city to live in. It has a young, energetic, highly educated population clustered around its three universities and the Research Triangle Park. It has great cultural events, including the American Dance Festival, the Full Frame Documentary Film Festival, the Durham Performing Arts Center, the Nasher Museum, and the wealth of events sponsored by its universities. It has great food, rooted in southern tradition and flavored by a booming local organic farming industry. It has open spaces, hiking and biking trails, funky retail areas, beautiful historic neighborhoods, artists and potters, writers and musicians in residence. All that, and it's affordable. In many ways, Durham and its neighbor communities of Chapel Hill, Raleigh, Carrboro and Cary seem to have struck the perfect balance of urban amenities and small-town livability. For most of us residents, the regular articles in the back pages of the newspaper about another shoot-

1

ing, another dead body found in the street are little more than background noise. They make us feel vaguely uneasy. We worry about our own safety. But then the police reassure us that we shouldn't worry too much. Most of the murders take place in a few troubled blocks of East Durham. It's basically just gang members shooting other gang members in neighborhoods where we never need to go. To quote the Police Department, "Public opinion polls last year [2007] indicated that by 8 to 1 Durham residents feel safe in their own community and that by 8 to 1 they feel safe in their own neighborhoods ... information and perceptions of Durham are often exaggerated by generalizing problems in parts of town to the community as a whole."[2]

My own impression is that the problem of gun violence in Durham is not exaggerated. On the contrary, it is minimized. It is minimized because the city wants to put a good spin on its image. And it is minimized also because the group who it affects the most — poor black young men — are all but invisible. Alongside the affluent, diverse, upwardly mobile, fun-loving majority population of Durham, there is a group whose poverty and dislocation are so extreme that they might be living in a third-world country. Less than half of African American men in Durham complete high school. In one survey, over 40 percent of middle school boys had carried a weapon in the past year. Ninety-one percent of youths appearing before the juvenile court were African American. In some districts, 116 families out of every thousand were being investigated for child abuse or neglect. Only 50 percent of elementary and middle school students were performing at their grade level, and 81 percent of the students identified as behaviorally or emotionally handicapped were black.[3] In 2009, the lowest fifth of Durham families had household incomes averaging only $11,000 per year.[4]

There is nothing particularly extreme about Durham. Statistics similar to these could probably be found in most medium-sized cities in the American South. Durham's "problem" is not a local problem. It is an American problem. It is, fundamentally, the problem of inequality, discrimination, and lack of opportunity.

But what to do about it? Like most of my friends in the Durham community, I worried about the existence of this frightening anomaly in our midst, but felt helpless to change anything.

And then I met Marcia Owen.

Marcia is the founder of the Religious Coalition for a Nonviolent Durham. I think of her as Durham's Mother Teresa. She comes from a perfectly ordinary background in the ranks of Durham's white middle classes. After attending high school in Durham she went away to college, married, and lived and worked in the Northeast for fifteen years. Then, in her middle thirties, she returned to Durham. She was horrified by the transformation that she found. During the years she was away, it was as though the low-income black population had been sliced right out of the city's heart. So effectively had they been shunted aside by the upwardly mobile majority that their presence was barely recognized. Meanwhile, the marginalized minority population had descended into a world of horrific violence, fueled by gang culture and the ready availability of guns.

"I just realized that I couldn't live another day while my brothers and sisters were dying," she told me. Driven by a deep Christian faith, Marcia has devoted herself heart and soul to alleviating the problems of violence and injustice that plague Durham's core. For Marcia, devotion is not just about organizing. It's about serving the needy on a daily basis. Her schedule is as crowded as a chief executive's, but instead of budget meetings and marketing plans, she spends her day testifying in court on behalf of mothers whose children are about to be taken away; delivering food to families that can't hold out till the end of the month; driving a mother whose son has been murdered to jail to visit another son who is himself accused of murder; pleading with her congressman for support of a new program; making presentations to the church congregations of Durham and telling them that yes, they can make a difference. They can just show up. They can just come to a vigil or a memorial service and show that they honor the common humanity of the poor and underprivileged people of East Durham. They can just show that they care.

As a historian I am used to writing stories, and after meeting Marcia and attending some of the vigils, it occurred to me that perhaps I could tell some of the stories of these victims — tell them in such a way as to show the humanity, the love that when I attended the vigils I could so obviously see was present in the victims' lives. I thought that by putting these stories in writing, I might bring some small comfort to the families;

I might create a more permanent memorial than the flowers and home-made crosses that adorned the sites of their killings. And I thought that if anyone were to read these stories, they might become more aware — aware of the humanity of the victims, of the love they had shared and the lives they had lived before they became a statistic in the daily crime report printed on an inside page of the *Herald-Sun*.

And so Marcia introduced me to Emma, a woman whose son had been beaten and shot to death in a derelict parking lot one year earlier.

I had originally only intended to ask Emma about her son. I wanted to tell Michael's story, not Emma's. But as we talked about Michael, I came to realize that if we are truly to understand the apparently senseless toll of violence in Durham and hundreds of other communities like it, we must look beyond the individual stories of life and death. We must look at the society that gave rise to these stories. We must look at the families, their economy, their culture. We must try and understand not only how the conditions for violence arose, but how our society created them.

And so I began meeting with Emma regularly in her small house in East Durham, as she slowly recounted the story of her difficult and eventful life.

Our project called on both of our reserves of patience. Emma suffers from a variety of serious health problems. She takes a bewildering array of prescription drugs, some of which leave her groggy and uncommu-nicative. We had to cancel at least one meeting out of two because of these issues. Moreover, as we worked together, Emma became embroiled in a variety of family dramas. Her pregnant daughter was run over. Another daughter was on the run from the police. Her granddaughter was pregnant and homeless. Several times, Emma's financial troubles became overwhelming and forced her attention away from the project.

Even when we were able to talk, there was so much about her life that I could not easily understand. Emma and I could hardly be more different. I am a college professor, raised in England, a transplant like so many others in twenty-first-century Durham. Emma was forced to leave school in the eighth grade. She was born in Durham, and she has lived here virtually her entire life. I am financially secure, and I live a life of richly rewarding work and pleasant society. Emma struggles to put food on the table from month to month. She is immobile and often

4

lonely. Emma is only eight years older than me, but she is a great-grand-mother (my children are still in their teens). She is sustained by deep religious faith, while I am more or less an atheist. I travel frequently, while Emma has never been on a plane and in recent months has hardly set foot outside her own house. We both speak the English language, yet I often have to ask her to repeat a phrase three or four times before I can understand her.

And yet, in spite of all these difficulties and differences, something happened between me and Emma. The simplest word for it is friendship. Across the chasm of our different experiences, we reached toward each other to find the common ground of human experience. I came to realize that Emma is not really so different from me. She has the same desires, the same anxieties, the same urge to make a difference in the world. She is intelligent, articulate, astute. And indeed, considering the disadvantages she has suffered, Emma's achievements are nothing short of astounding. As Emma shared her story with me, I realized that I had a vast amount to learn from her — about living amidst adversity; about looking on one's past with humor and wisdom; about dignity in the face of a lifetime of discrimination and denied opportunity; and about sustaining the values of love, friendship, and humanity in the face of overwhelming trials. As we worked together on "our project," I believe our relationship deepened into something profoundly meaningful for both of us. Knowing Emma Johnston has added to the rich-ness of my life in ways that I had not imagined possible. It has been an honor and a privilege to work on this story with her.

What did we hope to achieve by telling this story? Both of us felt it was important — something worth putting many hours into, even though we had no idea if it would ultimately be published. Emma per-haps put her side of it best in an article she wrote for the Durham *Her-ald-Sun*, to which she has been contributing for the past ten years.

> *Some of us think that we are owed something, that life is supposed to take care of us. If only one person can read about how I live and the lessons I learn on a daily basis ... then I have accomplished some-thing important.*

I am a professional historian, and Emma's story is history. It is, in fact, the third book I have written that narrates the story of an individual who otherwise would be forgotten by history (the other two were both Japanese). I think this is an important mission, because these are the people who had to *live* the history that famous and powerful people *made*. In Emma's case, the history that she lived was that of the postwar American South. Her story illustrates a side to her community's history that is not usually found in the published sources, which have tended to portray upward trajectories of increasing wealth and opportunity, victories in the civil rights movement, and the flourishing of a diverse culture. Emma's trajectory has not been upward. Her children and grandchildren today are facing many of the same problems — problems of segregation and discrimination, problems of poverty, and problems of violence — that Emma herself grew up with.

Then, by using material both from Emma's life and from the postwar history of Durham, I wanted to draw some connections between the social and economic conditions of Emma's birth, childhood, and adulthood, and the many harsh and tragic events that have befallen her, culminating in the murder of her deeply loved son. Emma's life has been her own to live, and she stands ready to take responsibility for her wrong choices. But her life has also been shaped by a society —*our* society — that systematically deprived her of opportunity from birth onward; a society that forced her and her children into deeply segregated systems of housing and education; a society that treated crimes against poor black people as less weighty than crimes against middle-class whites; a society that has often treated its poor, minority members as though they were invisible. I wanted to show Emma's relationship to that society. I wanted to show the moments in her life when she had the ability to choose her path, but also the moments when she just had to accept the legacies that she inherited by virtue of being born poor and black in the American South.

And third, I wanted in telling this story to convey my sense of the *worth* of Emma's life. For me, the experience of writing this book has been an experience of shared humanity, of the universal light of the human spirit. Discovering Emma's humor, intelligence, and great wisdom was a wonderful, unexpected bonus. Emma has a great story to tell, a story that's as meaningful, as instructive, as human as the biography of any politician or business magnate.

Thank you, Emma, for sharing it.

A word on the writing. I wanted as much as possible to tell Emma's story in her own words. But I did not want to be just a ghost writer. I thought, and Emma agreed, that I could add useful perspective by also including my own voice in the narrative. I wanted to tell not only Emma's story, but also the story of Durham and its African American communities. And I wanted to add a little analysis, to try and understand how Durham's history — and that of the American South — has affected Emma's life. And so we decided on the hybrid structure of this book — my narration, with extensive use of Emma's voice in italics. I was the scribe, but Emma, who is herself an accomplished writer, was deeply involved in the writing process. She reviewed every page of every chapter, often multiple times, and so ultimately we share authorship of the book. I, however, take responsibility for any errors in the historical research that underpins the book.

We agonized over what to do about names. As much as possible we wanted to tell a true story, down to the specific details. We went over many of those details — of events that took place decades ago — time and again, to iron out inconsistencies and to ensure that as much as possible the stories adhered both to Emma's memory and to the documented historical record. But in the end we decided to change almost all of the names of both people and places, including Emma herself. Many of the stories in the book are painful, and many of the participants still living. Some of the most painful events described in the book relate to Emma's own children. All of them are aware of the content of the book and agree that it is important to have this story told, but we wanted to protect their identities as much as possible. Only the names of public figures, or of larger streets and neighborhoods, have been left unchanged. In order to protect Emma's identity, I have also omitted the specific dates of her published articles. All the extracts from Emma's articles are copyright by the Durham Morning Herald Co. and are reprinted with permission.

Many people have helped in the writing and publication of this book. We would like to thank in particular Marcia Owen of the Religious Coalition for a Nonviolent Durham; Lynn Richardson of the North Carolina Collection, Durham County Library; Bob Ashley of the Durham *Herald-Sun*; Sy Mauskopf and Bill Chafe of the Duke University Department of History; Jerry Gershenhorn of the NCCU Department of History; and Elaine Maisner of UNC Press.

Chapter 1

A Hayti Childhood

In July 1950, the eyes of the world were riveted on the dramatic setbacks being suffered by American and United Nations troops on the Korean Peninsula. A terrible war had begun less than a month earlier. Korean troops had crossed the artificial border with the south on June 25, and by June 28 they had captured Seoul. The South Korean regime was on the brink of annihilation. America entered the war on June 27 and fought its first military engagement on July 4. But American involvement could not stop the relentless push of the northern forces, right down to the southern tip of the Korean Peninsula. It wasn't until northern troops were at the gates of Pusan, Korea's southernmost city, that the South Korean and American allies were able to hold the line.

In the city of Durham, North Carolina (population 73,000), the Korean conflict seemed far away. True, American troops were being mobilized throughout the country, many of them concentrating in nearby Fort Bragg before shipping out to the Far East. And true, young American men were still subject to the draft, which might call them up to fight half a world away in a conflict that few understood and even fewer believed in. But for most inhabitants of Durham, the brutal heat of a July afternoon was far more real than the distant struggle against the forces of international Communism.

The tobacco crop was real. The first tobacco of the season was coming into town on trucks and dray carts, the farmers sitting on top of their loads of tightly bundled leaves, ready to sleep on the warehouse floor until their merchandise could be sold at one of the half dozen auctions held in the various warehouses around the town. The heat was real. The July temperatures climbed up near one hundred degrees, and the people of Durham, black and white, sat listlessly on their porches sipping cold drinks, their glasses sweating almost as much as their flushed faces.

9

The newspaper reported affairs both great and small. An officer of the U.S. Air Force announced the reconstitution of the wartime Durham Civil Air Patrol, with the aim of training local youths "on matters pertaining to the maintenance of air supremacy" of the United States. A committee of sixty-five delegates from Durham and other communities met in Greensboro to plan the defense of two black cousins who had been sentenced to death for the alleged murder of a white taxi driver. The Durham City Council met to discuss a final agreement with the newly constituted Durham Housing Authority, which was preparing to build the first of six hundred public housing units in the city. Movies were advertised at the Uptown, Astor, Center, Carolina, and Rialto theaters. For black people, the Booker T. Theater was showing *Men of Texas*. In Washington, Senator Lodge called on the Senate for immediate mobilization of American manpower and industry, and a speedup in rearming Western Europe, to block Russian aims for world domination. Within the next three years Lodge envisioned expansion of the Korean conflict, followed by Russian seizure of the Ruhr and Japan and an atomic attack on the United States.

Amidst these dramas, the birth of a baby in the segregated Lincoln Hospital passed completely without notice. Anna Lee Johnston, a 33-year-old worker in the American Tobacco Factory, endured the pain of childbirth with the stoicism that women have summoned since the dawn of the human race. As for the baby, who that same day was to receive the name Emma Sue Johnston, no one asked her how she felt about the agonizing journey from the comfort of the womb through the uterine passage and out into the harsh incandescent light of the delivery room.

Durham in 1950 was a city with an exciting past and an even more exciting future. For the past five decades, migrants had been pouring into the city to take advantage of its growing industries. Since the turn of the century the city's population had grown from seven thousand to over seventy. The undisputed king of Durham's industrial growth was the tobacco industry.

Tobacco had built Durham, from a railway depot of less than two thousand inhabitants in the mid-nineteenth century to the flourishing industrial city of the mid-twentieth. The heart of the city was home to tobacco auction houses, tobacco warehouses, tobacco processing facilities, and tobacco and cigarette factories. The downtown area supported a variety of service businesses that had grown around the tobacco industry and its workers: insurance, banking, hotel accommodation, and entertainment. And on the edge of the city, ancillary industries had grown to support tobacco production: textile factories to manufacture the bags used to store and ship tobacco, coopers' shops to make the wooden casks used for curing, and printers to manufacture the cigarette papers and packaging. And all of these industries had grown and prospered and diversified, so that Durham was now one of the most dynamic manufacturing centers in the Southeast.

To the west of the tobacco district was Duke University, a large and prestigious institution that was largely funded with tobacco money. To

Lincoln Hospital. By the time Emma was born here in July, 1950, Durham's African American hospital had been operating at this site for twenty-five years. Financed by public contributions matched by the Duke family, the hospital boasted a school for black nurses, and a staff of mainly black doctors Note the curved window screens, which make the windows appear to bulge from the building. (North Carolina Collection, Durham County Library).

the east was North Carolina College, one of only two black colleges in the state of North Carolina — it, too, had received substantial support from tobacco money, as had the Lincoln Hospital in which baby Emma came into the world, and the Watts Hospital, the white people's hospital on the other side of town.

The whole story of growth and development was largely built on the success of one family. George Washington Duke had emerged from the hardscrabble life of a homesteading tobacco farmer to become the king of Durham's boom industry in the late nineteenth century. His son, James Buchanan Duke, built on this hard-won success to create an empire beyond even his father's dreams. Through a series of brilliant investments buying out competitors and installing the latest cigarette-making machinery, "Buck" Duke built the American Tobacco Company into the largest tobacco concern in the world, at one time accounting for more than 90 percent of all cigarette sales in the United States. As a result of antitrust lawsuits, American Tobacco was eventually split up into four separate companies, of which two — American Tobacco and Liggett and Myers — remained in Durham. Durham remained one of the biggest tobacco manufacturing centers in the country.

The tobacco industry grew through the twentieth century with the advance of mass consumption and mass marketing. The manufacturers quickly discovered that an addictive product like the cigarette was an ideal vehicle for the developing techniques of marketing and advertising, and brands like Lucky Strike and Pall Mall became household names throughout the nation. The industry also turned out to be remarkably recession proof. Even the great slump of the 1930s barely slowed its growth; and the outbreak of war in 1941 brought on the biggest boom in the industry's history as demand for cigarettes surged among the far-flung military forces.

By many standards, Durham was ahead of other southern cities in the development of its black community. During the first half of the twentieth century, black businessmen — often supported by the white tobacco interests — developed some of the most successful black-owned companies in America, including the Mechanics and Farmers Bank and the North Carolina Mutual Life Insurance Company. Durham boasted a black high school and the only taxpayer-funded liberal arts college for blacks in the nation. The Hayti district, where more than half the city's black community lived, contained over one hundred independently owned black businesses and stores, including beauty parlors, restaurants, hotels, and theaters. During World War II, Hayti had been a magnet for the 40,000 servicemen housed in the newly constructed Camp Butner, fifteen miles away. Special bus routes were set up to bring soldiers into Durham, and thousands of them poured into the city in search of entertainment. In Hayti, they were offered a heady mixture of jazz music, moonshine liquor, "chitterling dinners, high class prostitutes, and crap games."[1] As one resident recalled, the soldiers were willing to "pay double for everything they get, only they want it right now."[2]

The Dukes were enormous benefactors to the city they had built. In addition to the direct economic benefits from the jobs and economic activity they created, they also contributed to countless local causes, great and small. The greatest of these was Duke University, which grew with Duke money from a local Methodist college into one of the world's great universities. During the 1920s, James Buchanan Duke donated over $40 million to the university to build a huge new campus, in the gothic style of an English medieval college. The gothic tower of the Duke chapel soared over the woods of southwest Durham, where it was built literally out of the forest.

And the university pointed to Durham's extraordinary future. By the mid-twentieth century, Durham was no longer just a tobacco boomtown. Its industries had become diversified, and the combined brain power of Duke, North Carolina College, the University of North Carolina in nearby Chapel Hill, and North Carolina State University in Raleigh brought together one of the premier educational and intellectual communities in the Southeast. Already, medical and agricultural research was bringing new industries to the region, and America's tobacco heartland was coming to be known as the Research Triangle. Growth and economic buoyancy have been the insignia of Durham's twentieth-century history.

Emma's parents had met in the upheavals of the early postwar period. Her father, Jacob Johnston (known to his friends as Kingfish), had been in the military and had passed through Durham in the process of demobilization. Anna, Emma's mother, worked in the American Tobacco factory, and when the two of them married, Jacob stayed on in Durham.

Duke Chapel, 1930s. The chapel was the keystone of the ambitious West Campus development financed by James Buchanan Duke. Completed in 1935 at a cost of $2.3 million, the chapel was a symbol of Duke's grand vision even in the darkest days of the Depression (Library of Congress, LC-J7-NC-2341).

Anna was one of the economic migrants who had poured into Durham throughout the past five decades. She was born in 1917 in Bennettsville, South Carolina. She was one of five siblings, born into a poor laboring family on the outskirts of a poor and depressed town. Anna's lot was especially hard. Both of her parents, Adelaide and Richard Johnson, died while the children were still young. Her older brother, Evander, was fourteen, and Anna just twelve. In a land of limited opportunity and minimal welfare, the two oldest children had to take responsibility for supporting their three younger siblings. Unable to manage on their own, they moved to Wilson, North Carolina, where they had an uncle and aunt. But their relatives could not care for all of them, and a few months later, Anna moved to Durham, to stay with another uncle,

Jimmy, and his wife Martha. Uncle Jimmy was a kind soul with a heart of gold, but Aunt Martha was mean and harsh with her new charge. She had no intention of supporting a hungry child. Uncle Jimmy wanted to enroll Anna in elementary school (it was the first and only school she ever attended), but after only two weeks, Aunt Martha pulled her out and marched her to the American Tobacco factory, where they put her to work on the stemming floor. Anna worked alongside hundreds of other black women laborers ranging from ten to eighty years old. Her aunt expected her to hand over her wages as soon as she received them, and Anna was lucky if she got even a wedge of corn bread for her lunch.

> *It was abuse, but they just didn't have a name for it in those days. The people in the factory were very sympathetic to her. Even the bosses went out of their way to do little things for her. They tried to be a buffer between Ms. Martha and my Mama. They taught her how to put away money without letting Ms. Martha know. That's why she was so rooted in the American Tobacco family.*

As soon as she could, Anna moved out of her aunt's house and got her own place to live. Soon after, she sent for her younger brother Rufus and her sister Mary. She took care of both of them until they were grown up, at which point Mary got married and Rufus enlisted in the navy. During all this time, Anna remained unmarried. It wasn't until she was close to thirty years old that she met the man who was right for her.

While her brothers and sisters went on to have large families — Mary had thirteen children, and another brother, Herbert, had fourteen — Anna and her husband had only three children. After Emma they had two sons, Lionel and Henry. Emma was born in 1950, Henry (known in the family as Junebug) in 1952, and Lionel, the youngest, in 1955.

The Durham that Emma was born into was a community of strictly separate spheres for blacks and whites. The segregation of blacks and whites was the product both of law and economic circumstance. North Carolina was a full-blown Jim Crow state. State laws mandated segregation in the schools, on public transportation, and in the waiting rooms and toilets of public facilities. Interracial marriages were strictly prohibited. Negroes were forced to submit to a literacy test before they were allowed to exercise their right to vote (whites were excused by a "grand-

15

father" provision: anyone whose ancestors had been registered to vote prior to the abolition of slavery remained eligible). In one egregious case in 1936, two black college graduates with teaching certificates were barred from voting under the literacy test by a voting registrar. When they demanded a reason, the registrar simply replied, "You do not satisfy me." The state Supreme Court upheld the registrar.[3] Only with the Voting Rights Act of 1965 were such rules made explicitly illegal. One study estimated the percentage of eligible blacks who were registered to vote at 10 percent in North Carolina in 1940, 38 percent in 1960, and still only 55 percent in 1970.[4]

Durham city ordinances and local custom filled the gaps in state law. In restaurants, the city code required "separate rooms for the separate accommodation of each race. The partition between such rooms shall be constructed of wood, plaster or brick or like material, and shall reach from the floor to the ceiling."[5] Local ordinances and custom also mandated separate seating in theaters, hotels, water fountains and public restrooms, jails, prisons, hospitals and sanatoriums (even donated blood was kept segregated),[6] barber shops and beauty parlors, churches, elevators, entrances to buildings, athletic facilities, pool halls, Masonic lodges, Boy and Girl Scout groups, 4-H clubs, YWCA branches, insane asylums, swimming pools, and lakes for fishing and boating.[7] Separate libraries were maintained for blacks and whites, and if blacks wanted a book that was in the white Durham Public Library, they had to request it through interlibrary loan.[8] Parks, too, were segregated into "white" and "Negro" parks. The city's fifteen white parks and playgrounds totaled 174 acres, compared with 33 acres for the eight Negro parks. Whites had three swimming pools compared to one for blacks.[9]

Of the eight movie theaters in Durham, four — the Astor, Criterion, Rialto, and Uptown — were all-white and would not allow blacks to enter. Two, the Regal and Booker T., both on Pettigrew Street in Hayti, were all-black. Two other white-owned theaters, the Center and the Carolina, allowed blacks but required them to enter by a separate door and to sit in the upper balconies, known locally as the "buzzard roost."[10]

The railway station had separate waiting rooms for whites and blacks, with the ticket office and magazine stand in the middle. Blacks often had to wait until all the whites on the other side were served before they could buy their tickets. Once on the train they were seated in separate cars, and if they wanted to eat in the dining car, they were made to sit in a designated area, which was then curtained off from the rest of the dining car. The segregation was mandated by state law.[11]

For Emma, segregation meant growing up in a world that was almost exclusively black. Her street, East Spence, in one of the poorest sections of the Hayti neighborhood, was of course black. Housing was segregated by custom, and the five census tracts that constituted the Hayti neighborhood contained barely a single white family.

The black concentration of Durham was not in fact a normal pattern for urban areas in the South, where blacks and whites tended to live in scattered communities side by side. The entire black community of Durham lived in just five neighborhoods (Hayti, East End, Walltown, Hicksville, and Lyon Park). In part these dense concentrations were the product of black entrepreneurship. Most of the land in the Hayti area

At the bus station in Durham, 1940. This arresting photograph of Durham's segregated bus station was taken in 1940 by Jack Delano, working for the Information Division of the New Deal–financed Farm Security Administration. The bus and train stations were just one feature of Durham's rigidly segregated way of life (Library of Congress, LC-USF33-020522-M2).

had been purchased by W.G. Pearson early in the century, and he developed the land into an exclusively black community. However, the white community certainly encouraged the segregation. Housing advertised in the newspapers was clearly labeled if it was intended for "colored" residents, and it was quite common for deeds of property in upper-class white neighborhoods to include racial segregation clauses prohibiting future sale to blacks.[12]

The men, women and children who surrounded Emma were black — the elderly couple whom she thought of as her grandparents; the succession of neighbor women who took care of Emma and her brothers while their mother was at work; the men who came home exhausted after long days in the factories and construction sites, or who gathered outside the post office early in the morning to be hired by the day; the unemployed who stood or sat around the porches of the old frame houses and drank liquor out of brown paper bags; the mothers, aunts, and grandparents of her childhood friends, who would take Emma in and feed her like a member of their own family, but who also would not hesitate to scold her like their own child; the shopkeepers on nearby Pine Street; the employees of the Peter Pan grocery store, the nearest thing to a supermarket in Emma's neighborhood; the delivery boys who wove their way along the dirt streets, among the puddles; the schoolteachers, janitors, librarians and cafeteria workers; and the pastor and congregation in St. Mark's African Methodist Episcopal Zion Church, on the corner of Pine Street and Lakewood Avenue. The family's places of entertainment were black, too: the illegal liquor shops where Anna would drink a few shots after her long day at the factory; the informal clubs with their piccolo jukeboxes and basement card games; and the Regal Theater on Pettigrew Street, screening movies featuring the black film stars of the day.

Emma's world was so comprehensively black that she was barely aware of the existence of white people. Certainly, Mr. Magolia who ran the corner shop where they sometimes bought their supplies was white. But he was so much a part of the local landscape that Emma did not even register him as different from the other faces around her — indeed it never occurred to her that his children, who came with him to the store and played all day with the black children of the neighborhood, were any different from her.

18

St. Mark's AME Zion Church. St. Mark's African Methodist Episcopal Zion church was founded in 1890 by the Reverend C.H. McIver. The present structure was built in 1954 and reflects the relative prosperity of Hayti's African American community. Emma was a regular attender at the church throughout her childhood (Simon Partner).

The "meat man" who traveled the neighborhood in his beaten-up old station wagon carrying live chickens and cuts of pork and chitterling was definitely white. So were the insurance salesman and the "Watkins man," who drove round the neighborhoods peddling bedspreads, household goods, white liniment, and medicines out of his car. But these were clearly outsiders, people whose arrival was always greeted by shouts and running feet among the neighborhood children.

The foremen in her mother's factory, where Emma occasionally had to go to deliver a message, were also white. But again, they were outside the neighborhood, outside the sphere of Emma's everyday life. The same may be said for the white sales men and women in the department stores of downtown Durham, where Anna would sometimes take Emma to shop at Baldwin's or Sears.

And because Emma's childhood was lived so exclusively among black

Children reading Sunday comics, Hayti district. Another photograph by Farm Security Administration photographer Jack Delano. Emma grew up with her two brothers in a house of similar size and quality, and with her love of reading she might well have been one of these children enjoying the early summer warmth on a lazy Sunday afternoon (Library of Congress, LC-USF33-020543-M4).

people, she did not grow up feeling the sting of the city's cruel segregation laws and customs. Emma's community was self-contained. She did not need to ride the buses, where she would be sent to sit in the back as a matter of course and of law. She did not visit the white schools, so she did not see how her own school had been starved of amenities to pay for the superior facilities that the white children enjoyed. She did not eat in the downtown restaurants, which were either closed to blacks altogether, or maintained separate seating areas for whites and blacks. On the occasions when her mother took her to the department stores, she did not notice that the white customers were allowed to try clothes on, while the black customers must make their purchase strictly on sight. And of course, she did not apply to white schools and universities, where boys and girls of her age were to struggle with the courts and the city elders for years to assert the right of equal access.

Emma's mother understood the realities of life as a poor black woman in a way that Emma would not know for years to come. For decades, black workers had been pouring into Durham — many of them like Anna from farms and small towns in South Carolina — to work in the Durham factories. The factories offered work to both black and white workers. However, the activities were for the most part segregated.

Black men manhandled the tobacco bales that came from the auction houses, stuffed the tobacco into hogshead barrels, and hauled the barrels to the warehouse for aging. Black women worked on the stemming floor, stripping the soft tobacco leaves from their hard, fibrous stems. The women would fold the large tobacco leaf along the stalk, holding the tip in one hand while grasping the stalk with the thumb and forefinger of the other. Then with a quick twist of the wrist, they would tear out the stalk. The key was to avoid tearing or creasing the leaf. The women had to stand throughout their nine-hour workday. While they worked they were encouraged to sing. Their songs could be heard outside the factory walls, prompting one observer to comment, "They were not singing for joy, but to ease the monotony of long hours going through the same motions day in and day out."[13]

The stemmed leaves were then put through a drying machine and a shredding machine — operated by black men — and sent up to the cigarette-making section of the factory. The cigarette machines were operated entirely by white girls. The machines would take the shredded tobacco, roll it in paper, print the brand on it, and cut it to size. Then they would wrap, package, and seal the cigarettes, and finally they would pack the cigarette boxes into cartons, which they would wrap and label. As one observer noted, "the work is so light and clean that it can easily be done by white girls. Only the weighing and handling of the final boxes is done by Negro men."[14]

By contrast, the work done by blacks was dusty and hot. The factory was not air-conditioned, and the dried tobacco shed a fine dust that filled the air in the stemming room. The smell of the tobacco was overpowering — it permeated the whole of central Durham — and for those with sensitive skin, the toxins given off by the leaves were a powerful irritant. But in spite of these conditions, there was a constant supply of willing workers for the 50-hour week. Anna would start work at seven and work

Tobacco stemming floor. The stemming floor was staffed entirely by African American women, who stood throughout their nine-hour shift as they stripped the toxic leaves. Amidst the heat, dust, and powerful smells of the tobacco factory, the women sang "not ... for joy, but to ease the monotony of long hours" (North Carolina Collection, Durham County Library).

all day with only a half-hour break until 4:30. Saturday was a half day. In her earlier days at the factory, Anna had been paid on a piecework basis: nine cents for every pound of leaves that she stemmed by hand. Now she was paid by the hour, but her wage was generally below the minimum wage ($0.80 an hour in the 1950s, $1 an hour at the turn of the 1960s). Workers could not expect any increase for seniority, and even the best-paid workers in the factory were low-paid by most standards. Indeed, many factory hands went on to other jobs after their factory workday just so that they could keep their families housed and fed.[15] Nor could Anna expect much in the way of benefits. The factory work was seasonal, with a busier season in the fall and a slack season in the winter and spring, when the factory would often slow down to a four-day week (smaller factories closed down altogether from January to July, hiring seasonal labor each year). Anna did not receive wages for the days on which the factory closed, nor did she receive any benefits in case she got sick. The company had no pension plan for black workers either, so men and women who had worked there all their adult lives might find themselves destitute in their old age. In the busy season, overtime work was compulsory. As one factory hand put it, "You have to work until 9 or lose your job. You have got to have a job, and you've got to stick to it."[16] One concerned observer remarked on the long hours: "They get up at 5:30, prepare their own breakfast and leave without even seeing their children. The draft is put on the fire so at 7:30 or 8:00 the oldest child gets up, cooks breakfast and looks after the younger children. He gets them off to school and sees that the pre-school children arrive at the home where they are to be cared for during the day. This leads to grave moral hazards as the older children often do not go to school, but get together and dance at their home while their parents are away.... Such houses are easy to spot in the daytime by the number of children playing in the street, and in and out and under the house."[17]

For any other kind of benefits, the workers were heavily dependent on the generosity of their foremen. As one factory hand said, "If he likes you and you are an old hand he may give you a little help" in the event of sickness or personal difficulty.[18] Many of the foremen were dyed-in-the wool racists, and they acted with their employers' encouragement. One boss was quoted as saying, "We keep our Negro labor as bound and subservient as possible because it doesn't pay to do otherwise." "Negroes have no intelligence," said another. "Only brute treatment appeals to them."[19] Women workers had to put up with verbal and sexual harassment. One worker remembered being cursed out by a one-eyed foreman who would stand on top of the machinery and "holler down and curse. Curse and we working.... You didn't say anything. You said anything, you went out."[20] Anna was lucky to have white foremen who took good care of her, and indeed this was perhaps the biggest factor tying her to her workplace for over thirty years.

Often, Anna would stop on the way home at one of the liquor houses in the neighborhood, staying long enough for two or three shots before returning home to take care of her children. These liquor houses were a fixture in the leisure culture of the community. Durham remained a "dry" city — the sale of liquor in private shops or restaurants was prohibited until the late 1970s — with the result that much of the liquor consumption took place in these underground venues. They provided significant income and independence for the women who ran many of them — many were influential community leaders — and they operated as informal centers of local black culture. They also, of course, promoted alcoholism and in that sense were "living testimonies to the debilitating effects of racism, poverty, and broken dreams."[21]

The children knew that their mother stopped to drink on the way home. But they looked out for her all the same.

> Mama had a coworker who always had candy, and every day Mama'd bring home some kind of treat for us. So we'd look out for Mama coming down the street after work, and when we saw her, we'd run to grab her pocketbook, because in the pocketbook was the candy. In the end, we shared it all, though.

After fixing dinner for her children, Anna would relax on the porch with visiting friends from the neighborhood, smoking unfiltered Pall Mall cigarettes and gossiping. On Saturdays she would go down to one of the neighborhood drinking houses, often coming back completely drunk and cursing like a sailor. But drinking was normal in the African American community of East Durham. Anna did not allow her drinking to get in the way of her parental responsibilities.

Flower seller, downtown Durham. This poetic photograph taken in the heart of downtown Durham hides the harsh economic realities that forced African American children to seek a living when they should still have been in school (Library of Congress, LC-USF33-020514-M2).

On Saturday nights Emma's mother would work in the kitchen getting a full southern meal ready for the following day. Then on Sunday morning, she would take her family to St. Mark's Church.

Then they would return home for what they called "Sunday meats." The children would stuff themselves on fried chicken and picnic ham, greens, and macaroni and cheese, as well as southern treats like pig's feet, pig's ears, and oxtails. For dessert there were stewed apples with cinnamon, or apple pie or cobbler.

Although Anna was busy, she managed to find the time and resources to give her children a safe and secure upbringing.

Looking back, I can see that we had a real sense of security. We had so many people watching out for us, no matter what we did. You were known, your family was known, you couldn't get away with too much. The families relied on one another. Looking back, it was wonderful. I'm so glad I had that. It shaped who I am and how I view things. It made me feel stronger. No matter if I didn't have a lot of money, I could still bring my kids up and not give up. You know, my mother was a special kind of person. She showed her love in thousands of ways. My friends wished they could trade places with me. But she did expect you to be respectful and obedient. "I can't stand a sassy child," she'd say. If you talked back, that was sassy. It took a lot to get her to punish you, but when she said she would, she did. She was good at plaiting switches, even though she couldn't plait my hair the way I wanted it!

Emma's earliest years in this community were happy. She had little sense that her family was poor — there was always food on the table, and the children did not lack for any essentials. Emma had a bicycle from an early age, and at Christmas the tree was always well supplied with presents. She knew that her mother worked at a harsh job, but the factory was a world that Emma seldom had to confront. She knew that she could expect a spanking from any one of a dozen neighbors if she was caught doing something wrong. But she also knew that she would be taken in and fed, comforted, and protected by those same neighbors. She knew that her mother liked to get drunk occasionally on the weekend, and her father was often visited by unsavory friends, but she adored her parents all the same. With the birth of her two brothers, she had a family — a family that for all its status at the lowest level of American society was a place of love and caring.

During her first six years, Emma made only one long trip — to Louisiana, to meet her paternal grandparents. Her grandmother, Pauline, had been sending packages of food, clothes and toys to the family since Emma was a baby.

That was how I got to taste Creole cooking. It was very spicy. She'd send hog head sausage — it was a long sausage, full of herbs and seasonings. It tasted so different from our food here in Durham.

Now, her father took her to meet Grandma Pauline in person. Emma was deeply impressed by the Creole culture that she encountered there.

My grandma was so regal — but loving, too. She had a lot of French-speaking friends. It was a strange language to me — my father would have to tell me what the people were saying. They knew English and Creole, and my father also knew Spanish. I have no idea why. I just remember that my father used to shave his head, and

*every two weeks he'd go to the barber to get it shaved. The barber
would shave it with a cut-throat razor, just like he'd shave your face.
He'd do Daddy's face and head too, and trim his mustache. Anyway,
my Daddy had to interpret for me when I went there with him. And
he told me that the barber was a Spaniard. They had all these inter-
esting people in their lives — but of course, to them it was ordinary.*

Emma's world was supportive and nurturing, and her early childhood was happy and secure. But the society she was born into was vulnerable, torn at times by harsh forces of violence and disintegration. The
economic want, the lack of education, the joblessness, the dependency
on liquor to drown out the cares of a harsh world, all contributed to
inject a dark vein into Emma's environment. Drink and violence were
constantly in the background of her own life and those of the neighboring
families. And indeed, Emma's years of happiness were to be short-lived.

In addition to his job in the Liggett and Myers tobacco factory,
Emma's father was one of dozens of men in the neighborhood who traded
in illegal liquor, and for a while he and Anna also offered shots of liquor
out of their house, turning it into an illegal bar. The police were generally
lenient with illegal drinking in Hayti, and dozens of liquor houses operated with little trouble from the authorities. But they did crack down
now and again on the suppliers, and Kingfish had been caught up in
their raids on several occasions. In 1956, his difficulties with the law
resulted in the sudden breakup of Emma's family.

*My Daddy didn't just walk out on us. He felt if he didn't leave
he'd be going to prison. He'd been arrested before, and this time,
they'd have sent him to prison for sure. He wanted to take us all with
him, but my mother said no.*

Anna had been working at American Tobacco since she was thirteen
years old, and she was known and respected there. In another city, she
would be an illiterate nobody, dependent on her husband for her livelihood.

Emma's parents remained legally married. But as the years went by,
they went on with their separate lives. Anna kept working at the tobacco
factory and supporting her family on her wages. For a while she continued
selling liquor out of her house, but she was always nervous about the

men who would come in for shots before work in the morning and again in the evening. Even after giving up that side activity, though, she always managed to put food on the table for her children, and they felt little of the poverty that was their unknowing reality.

If my mother had had the chance to go to school, her life would have been much different. She worked, she kept her house clean, she took care of her children — she was like a little warrior to me. Whatever needed taking care of, she took care of it, even after I was married. She was my hero in a skirt!

Soon after her father's departure, Emma enrolled in the first grade in the W.G. Pearson elementary school. This school was named after William Pearson, one of Durham's most influential black leaders. Pearson was born a slave in Durham, and during and after Reconstruction he

Pearson Elementary School. Built in 1928, the school for African American children was named after William Pearson, one of Durham's most influential black leaders and the major landlord of the Hayti district. In spite of the school's limited facilities in comparison with the city's privileged white schools, Emma spent the happiest days of her childhood here (© Durham Morning Herald Co. Reprinted with permission).

had witnessed firsthand the burning of black schoolrooms by white agitators who were determined not to allow black children to gain an education. Pearson was the original owner of much of the land that became Hayti, and during his lifetime he was the area's biggest landlord. But he was more than just a businessman. Pearson devoted much of his life to pioneering black education in Durham. For many years he served as principal of Whitted School and "by extension as the unofficial superintendent of all public black schools in Durham."[22] In the 1920s, there were nineteen privately run "colored" schools in Durham County, most of them operating in one-room schoolhouses with two or at most three teachers. The school facilities were cramped and inadequate, prompting one educator in the 1920s to comment that "if the school attendance law was enforced there would be no place to take care of the children."[23] During the early decades of the century, the Whitted School was the only black school to extend beyond fourth grade.

By the time that Emma started school, however, there were a total of eight city-financed black schools in Durham: six elementary schools, one middle school, and one combined middle and high school. This was compared to fourteen white schools, even though the total attendance at white schools was only 20 percent higher than at black schools. All of the teachers and staff in the black schools were African American, including the principals. However, all of the members of the county's board of education were white. The refusal of the city to appoint a black board member had been the subject of much controversy. During the 1940s, blacks had repeatedly complained about poor facilities and the arbitrary assignments and firings of teachers. In one particularly egregious incident, the board appointed a black principal of Hillside High School against the objections of the entire black community. They said that he was mentally unbalanced, cruel, and undemocratic. But an official complaint against the principal was dismissed as "communistic," and six of the ten teachers who submitted it were dismissed. Tragically, the principal proved his critics right when he killed his own son and then himself.[24]

Under the Jim Crow laws, North Carolina's constitution called for "separate but equal" facilities for white and black students. The reality, though, was a thoroughly unequal system, in which white schools were far more privileged than their black counterparts. The appraised value of Durham's white schools was $3.9 million, versus $1.3 million for the black schools. The white children had a total of 22 acres of land available to them on the combined school grounds, compared to four acres for the combined black schools. White children could enjoy the use of equipment worth $203 per student, compared with $51 for black children. A 1947 study of the city's school system observed that one of the black schools was on an unpaved street; it had no partitions between the girls' toilets; it had no lunch room; and the principal, "according to his own personal statement, doubles also as a school janitor."[25] Only one of the six black elementary schools had a music or art room. In several of the black schools students had to study in windowless and damp basement rooms, where they had poor ventilation and inadequate lighting. The black schools had few facilities beyond the basic classroom accommodations. Emma's school, with 937 students, could only seat forty children in its cafeteria at one sitting. None of the black schools had a gym.[26] Black schools received only $0.42 per student for every $1 per student that white schools received for library materials.[27] The school curricula also discriminated heavily against black students. White high school students could take classes in Latin, Spanish, geometry, government, and trigonometry — none of them available in the black schools — while black high school students were offered classes in automobile mechanics and "Sheet Metal."[28] No facilities were offered to black children with special needs. Student-teacher ratios were consistently higher in the black schools, and black teachers faced a much heavier teaching load than their white counterparts.

These differences were part of a comprehensive pattern of discrimination that pervaded every aspect of life for blacks in Durham and most other southern towns. Education was obviously not considered as important for black children as for white, and this bias was strengthened by the likelihood that black youths would leave school earlier than whites and end up in blue-collar jobs. Of course, the fact that white-owned companies in Durham never hired black clerks or salesmen, let alone managers, ensured that this cycle would be repeated.

But for Emma, school wasn't about the opportunities she was denied — she was blissfully unaware of those. School was about the joys of learning and friendship. Emma loved her school from the day she first set foot in it. She was a remarkably intelligent child, and she quickly learned to read and write — a skill that was especially important to her because it had been denied to her mother. Her classes and teachers were a constant joy, and the joy of learning was augmented by the joys of friendship. School opened up a whole new world of friends, including her new best friends Jessie, with whom she became inseparable, and Jackie, who was two or three years older.

Emma missed her father, but she had grown accustomed to life without him. Privately, she spun fantasies about how he would come back one day, to reunite the family and spoil Emma with gifts and attention. But it was a shock all the same when one day after school finished, she saw him waiting for her outside the school gates.

> *I was so excited, so amazed to see him. I can still remember seeing him, my heart was just beating, I was so excited. I just remember staring at him. It felt like goose bumps. It was like seeing a star that you really admired. It was so irregular to me to actually see him, it just blew me away.*
>
> *The truth is, I used to make up things about my dad to the other children. I didn't know it, but I really missed him so much. So I made stuff up. I pretended that he'd come to town, that he'd taken me to the movies. And here he was, really here!*

He was waiting in a car. Opening the door, he hugged her and ushered her into the passenger seat. It was like her dream coming true! And just like in her dream, her father took her to the movies. The two of them drove to Pettigrew Street, the central shopping area for the African American community, and watched a show at the Regal Theater, followed by a slice of pie at Mrs. Vie's restaurant.

But as they talked, little Emma slowly came to understand that her father had no intention of taking her back to her Durham home. Rather, he wanted to take her with him to Louisiana.

> *I loved him to death. But I couldn't imagine being without my mother. She was my only parent—she was all that I had by way of security. I didn't doubt that my father loved me. But my mother was the constant in my life. When my father saw how upset I got at the thought of leaving her, he took me back home. My Mama had been so worried about me when I didn't come home, she'd even called the*

police. At first she was so glad to see me, she cried. She wasn't given to crying normally, so I knew that this was a big deal. In fact, I felt like it was me that had upset her. They sent me outside while they talked, but I could still hear what they were saying to each other. It wasn't real nice. That made me feel even more as though I had done something wrong. I thought maybe he had been planning to stay, but now that I'd made them upset, he'd change his mind. That feeling stayed with me a long time. My mother didn't know to reassure me, to tell me that I hadn't done anything wrong.

And after that incident, Emma seldom saw her father again. She continued to write to him at her grandmother's house, and her grandmother would write back. Grandma Pauline's letters would favor Emma, the oldest and the only girl, above her brothers.

Sometimes she'd send me money orders. They were in my name, but of course I had no idea what a money order was, so I always gave them to my mother. She thought it was unfair that I should get all the money, so the two of us decided that we'd share it equally between the three of us children. Lionel still believes that the money was for all of us.

When Emma was seven, her mother began dating Gerard. Gerard was from Wilmington, in the coastal area of North Carolina. He was a kind and sensitive man, who quickly bonded with Emma and her brothers. They were thrilled when he packed his bags and moved into Emma's house on Spence Street. Emma had missed having a father to spoil and encourage her, and Gerard filled that role for her. Gerard was proud of Emma's accomplishments at school, and whenever she was acting in a school play or competing in a school competition, she could always rely on his being in the audience, cheering her on.

Gerard expanded Emma's horizons in other ways, too. For two summers running, he took Emma's whole family to his family farm near Wilmington to help out in the tobacco harvest. Emma was still too young to pick, but she was put to work tying the sheaves. She enjoyed getting to know Gerard's sister, Esme, and her husband, as well as his grandparents, who also lived on the farm. And she was thrilled to earn a little money to buy her school clothes for the coming year. Gerard had a son of his own who lived in Wilmington with his mother, but who visited occasionally.

Anna's house had three bedrooms. The boys slept in one room, Emma in another, and Anna and Gerard in the third. Although from the outside it may have appeared dilapidated, the house was reasonably comfortable and well equipped. Anna's steady income combined with Gerard's wages as a construction worker to bring in money for some comforts as well as the necessities. The house was one of the first on the block to have a television set. It had electric fans in the windows to keep the family cool, and a coal-burning stove in the living room for the winter months. The house had a front porch where Anna would sit with Emma on warmer evenings and comb out her daughter's hair, and a screened-in back porch where little Lionel could play without fear that he would stray out into the street. It also had a front and a back yard, though little grew on the muddy ground. The house was equipped with modern plumbing, hot water, and a bathtub — where after a visit from the traveling "meat man," Anna would sometimes keep live chickens.

> *WRAL radio station was always on with my Mama and Grand-mama's favorite gospel songs on in the background, while they yelled back and forth at us to get dressed and hurry so someone else could get in the bathroom or something, sometimes getting our names mixed up.*

In addition to Emma's nuclear family, there was almost always an extended family of friends and relatives visiting or staying in the house. Anna had brought up her younger brother Rufus and her sister Mary since they were small children, and Anna continued to be their first line of defense if they found themselves in difficult circumstances.

Rufus had been in the navy for some time, and after his discharge he had ended up in New York, where he had run into trouble with the law and ended up in jail. After his release, he drifted back to Durham and took up residence with his sister Anna. He slept out on the back porch, and he spent most of his time drinking and womanizing. Eventually he began going steady with one of his girlfriends, and he moved in with her. Almost as soon as Uncle Rufus left, Aunt Mary moved in. After growing up under Anna's care in Durham, Mary had married and moved to South Carolina. By the mid–1950s she had thirteen children. But in 1958 she left her husband and her enormous brood and fled to Durham. Mary found refuge in her sister's house for more than a year, until eventually she found a new boyfriend in Durham and set up house on her own.

Another addition to the family was a couple called Freddy and May. They were family friends of Anna's from her childhood in South Carolina, and in the mid–1950s they moved to Durham to try their fortune in the local industries. They were an older couple, and Emma was led to believe that they were her own grandparents. After a short period of living in Emma's house, they moved into their own place on Crest Street, just a short walk away. To Emma, Grandpa Freddy and Grandmama May were everything that real grandparents should be.

> *Mama and Grandmama were always talking and laughing in the kitchen. Grandmama cooked the biggest biscuits you ever saw. They were a meal in themselves.*

Freddy and May's new house became a refuge for Emma. She would run there to get away from troubles at home, and she would always find a warm welcome.

> *I would run over there when my Mama was fixing to give me a whupping. Grandmama would take one look at my face and say "You might as well tell me what you done did." And so then I'd tell her my side of the story, and if she believed me, then she'd help protect me from my Mama.*

Grandmama May loved to dip tobacco snuff. She would sometimes send Emma out to buy a supply for her — either Tuberose brand, or Railroad Mills. Emma would watch as May pulled out her lower lip and used a spoon to stuff a plug into the space between her lip and her teeth. After she had finished absorbing the snuff, she would spit a stream of brown juice into the dirt outside the house.

> *Don't ask me why, but watching Grandmama dip like that, I got to wanting to try some for myself. So one day when Grandmama wasn't looking, I took me a pinch of that stuff and I pulled out my lip like she did and stuffed it in. Well, I sat for a while with that plug in my mouth, waiting for something to happen. And after I'd*

been waiting a while, I got sleepy, and before I knew it I'd fallen asleep. And while I was asleep, I swallowed that tobacco! Well when I woke up I felt as sick as I ever had in my life. I was running to the bathroom every three minutes, bringing it all back up. Grandmama said, "I'm not even going to whup you. The snuff's whupping you for me!"

It wasn't until she saw Anna's birth certificate after her mother's death that Emma discovered Freddy and May were not her real grandparents.

Aunt Mary and "grandparents" Freddy and May were welcome additions to Emma's life. But Uncle Rufus was another story altogether.

We hated it when he came to our house. He treated us like an intrusion, like we had taken Mama from him. It was like a private war between us and him.

Both Emma and her brother Junebug were terrified of Uncle Rufus. He would pull Emma's hair hard, until clumps of it came out in his hand.

I think Uncle Rufus had a fierce jealousy when it came to my mother. She was the only Mama he could remember real good. Mama had children late in life, and until that time he'd had a monopoly of her. She would always help him out in the messes he would get himself into. I think he couldn't stand not being the center of her life anymore.

As for Junebug, Uncle Rufus had a special urge to torture his sensitive nephew. Emma's younger brother was different from other boys. From his earliest childhood, he was convinced that he should have been born a girl.

He liked my toys better than he liked his. When we played families he wanted to be the Mama. I never heard him say he was gay. He just acted like Junebug, and Junebug liked boys. Even after he grew up and graduated school, he still liked to dress like a woman sometimes.

Uncle Rufus picked on Junebug mercilessly, calling him a sissy and a "fag." While his sister was away at work, Uncle Rufus had absolute power over the terrorized children. He would beat them at the slightest excuse —

and it was obvious that he was enjoying it. Often, he would bring his friends over to the house, and they would drink together until they could barely move. And then Uncle Rufus would turn on the children for sport.

Even though Uncle Rufus loved to torment Junebug, he reserved his special attentions for Emma. He was cruel to her, and yet he seemed obsessed with her. He was always touching her, sometimes just uncomfortably, sometimes painfully. At first, Emma was hardly aware of what he was doing to her — she just knew that she wanted to stay as far away from him as possible. But one July Fourth, when Emma was eight years old, he sat her on his knee outside in the yard while the firecrackers were popping off around the neighborhood, and he put his hand down the inside of her pants.

After that incident, Uncle Rufus began molesting Emma regularly. She did her best to stay out of his way. She slept fully clothed, sometimes going to sleep in her brothers' room for protection. But at night, the sound she dreaded would come as he softly opened the door and began reaching into the bed to touch her. She went to stay with friends whenever she could. But she was vulnerable. Her mother was gone much of the time, either at work or drinking with her friends. For Anna, Rufus was a convenient resource — a free babysitter who allowed her to live a little more of her own life. Emma considered talking to Gerard, who she knew hated Rufus. One of their neighbors, Ms. Frances, also tried her best to alert Anna. "I watches Rufus, and I know that he's slick," she told Anna. But Anna did not want to know. She trusted her brother, who had been almost a son to her, and she refused to believe the worst about him.

Emma's home, which had been a place of safety and comfort, had become a trap from which she couldn't see any way out.

> *I couldn't stop the molestation. He had a way of trying to get you by yourself. He'd wait till I'd let down my guard a little at a time. I thought I didn't have to worry about nothing. And then...*

Soon, when her mother was away he no longer bothered to hide his intentions. His touching became more insistent, his need more urgent. But his physical attraction to Emma did not make him any kinder. Even as he abused her sexually, he also kept her in physical terror of a beating or some other act of cruelty.

Emma began to play a desperate game of cat and mouse with her uncle. On the days when she knew her mother would not be home, she did everything she could to stay away. Often she would stay with her best friend Jessie's Aunt Sally. Other times, she would hang around in the street until she heard her mother coming home. But her adversary had many advantages. His sister trusted him. If Emma ignored his instructions to come home early, Anna would chide her daughter: "How can Rufus protect you if you won't listen to what he says?" She still did not understand that it was Rufus from whom Emma needed protection.

Mama would go visit with her friends, and Rufus would say, "Don't worry, Anna, I'll keep 'em." That made my heart just drop. I know he didn't want to keep us. He didn't even like us. He'd whup Junebug and Lionel for the littlest things. He'd wrap a belt round his hand and beat them with it. He'd leave marks on them too. Him and Mama fought about that many times.

But still, Anna continued to trust her brother with her children.

One day, Emma had come home and was getting ready for bed. There was no sign of Uncle Rufus — she thought he must be off drinking with one of his girlfriends. It was only when she was sitting in the bath that her uncle suddenly appeared in the doorway.

I didn't know what he was going to do, but I knew it was something. I thought maybe he'd hit me while my clothes were off.

Closing the door behind him, Uncle Rufus handed Emma a towel and waited while she got out of the bath and dried herself off. All the time she was drying herself, she was looking for a place to escape. But her brothers were asleep in their bedroom, and the door to the bathroom was firmly closed. Uncle Rufus was talking to her, soft and smooth, not like his usual cruel self. And as he talked, he began touching.

Emma felt as though she had seen all of this in a dream. As the towel fell to the floor, she had never felt so helpless or alone.

Rufus's hand strayed over her body. Emma, eight years old, tried to fight the evil hands, tried to force them away from her body. But her uncle was much, much stronger than her. The more she tried to fight back, the more she saw her uncle smiling. He seemed to find her resistance even more enticing.

For all of her fear, for all of her resistance, for all of her knowledge of her uncle's evil, nothing prepared her for what came next. Emma knew next to nothing about sex. She had heard friends and family members talk about "doing the nasty," but she had no concrete idea of what it meant. Now, forcing Emma down onto the wet floor, Uncle Rufus began touching her in her most private places. He made no effort to be gentle — his fingers hurt, and he seemed to enjoy the look of pain on his niece's face. And then he pulled his pants down.

What happened next is forever seared in Emma's memory. Reeking of alcohol, his eyes bloodshot and clouded with evil, her uncle held her down on the wet bathroom floor while he forced himself inside her. Emma, an eight-year-old child, lay helpless as her body was torn with agonizing pain, shame, and hatred.

> *Even today, when I think about it, it feels like bile coming up from my stomach. That's the feeling I have. I have to pray about the way I feel. If there's anyone in the world to hate, it's him. And it's a lot for me to hate someone. But he was mean through and through. To me he was walking evil.*

Once Uncle Rufus had gratified his perverted desire, he was hungry for more. A situation that had been troubling now became downright terrifying. Emma knew that whenever she let down her guard, her uncle was always waiting for her. He was patient and sly. He would leave her alone if her aunt or grandmother were in the house. Even when Junebug and Lionel were around he would keep his hands off Emma, preferring to torment his young nephews. But he would look for his opportunities. Once Junebug and Lionel were asleep, once Anna was safely out at her drinking party, once Grandmama May was home with her husband, Rufus would strike. Emma would wake to the weight of his body on her bed.

"You're gonna do what you're told," he whispered in her ear. "Cause you know that if you don't or if you breathe a word about this I'm going to hurt your precious Mama. Yup. I'm going to take me a belt and strangle her. I know you believe me." And Emma did indeed believe him. She had seen too much of what he was capable of doing. She struggled against him, but once he had her on her own it was always a losing battle. Month after month, the rape continued. Emma's body became the scarred battleground of an evil man's desire and a young girl's struggle to defend herself.

She wanted more than anything to tell her mother and have this terrible secret burden lifted from her. But she could not bring herself to tell the full truth. Her uncle had effectively terrorized her. She believed that if she told on him, she and perhaps all of her family members would be terribly hurt, perhaps killed. She had come to realize that her uncle was capable of anything, even murder. And what's more, she could see in her mother's face a determination not to believe the worst about her younger brother, to whom she had been more of a mother than a sister. Rufus was a gifted liar, and he always had some reason to give for any behavior of his that upset his sister.

And so Emma was forced to endure. She was too defenseless even to feel outraged at her mother's betrayal. Later, though, she came to realize that this was the one time that her adored mother had let her down.

She just couldn't see the truth about her own brother. She'd raised him herself; he was almost like her child. It would hurt her so much to believe something like that about him. I only saw her at a loss a few times in her life. Even when they amputated her legs she kept up her spirit. But when she finally had to accept what her brother Rufus had done, that came near to breaking her. That, and the other thing I did.

Faced with this hopeless situation, Emma became quiet and withdrawn. She would sit for long hours on the porch, no longer rushing off to play with her friends like she used to. In fact, she was afraid to be with her friends because she no longer felt normal—and because she was scared that if they ever came to her house, they too might fall into her uncle's clutches.

But when Anna was at work or out drinking with her friends, and when Rufus was left alone in the house, then Emma knew to stay away for as long as she possibly could.

Her greatest refuge was Aunt Sally's house.

Sally was not a real aunt, though she was distantly related to Anna. Emma's real connection to her was through her best friend, Jessie. Emma and Jessie were inseparable. They walked to and from school together every day, they played together whenever they were allowed, they spun fantasies together, they laughed and they gossiped. She was as close to a sister as Emma would ever have. Aunt Sally was Jessie's mother's close friend, and since Jessie's mother was dysfunctional, consumed with alcohol and men, Aunt Sally offered the closest thing to a home that Jessie would find. Jessie often stayed with her aunt for weeks at a time. Emma was allowed to sleep over on weekends. For Emma, Aunt Sally's was a precious refuge from the misery and fear of her own home. She would often take her own brothers, and one or more of Jessie's seven brothers might also be staying there.

Aunt Sally loved her young relatives, but she was strict.

> She expected you to learn how to do female things in the right way. You couldn't just walk in and start talking. If Aunt Sally was talking and you came in and interrupted, her dog was trained to lift up its tail. Then if we hushed, that tail would go back down. If Aunt Sally got mad at us then she'd order us to go upstairs and take our panties down. All the neighbors would know from the hollering that we were getting a whupping. She'd whup us with a switch made of rope, plaited like hair, with a runner band at the end. It left marks, it sure did! It would sting like the dickens. And it would have to be on our bare behinds. Aunt Sally always said that she don't do whuppings over no clothes.

But in spite of Aunt Sally's strict ways, the girls loved staying with her. She spoiled them as well as beat them. Sometimes she would go out and buy half a gallon of ice cream for them, crumbling cookies and hot chocolate over it before serving it to the girls. Emma wondered if she spoiled them because she felt guilty about the beatings — not that Emma ever questioned the beating: it was just a part of the culture of Hayti. The children might be beaten for tearing a hole in their stockings, or for rumpling the clothes that they had put out for their Sunday best. All those closest to them felt free to beat them — Anna, Gerard, Aunt Sally, Uncle Rufus, even white Charlie Magolia, who owned the corner shop and sold to Emma's family on credit. One neighbor, Ms. Beda, would spank Emma just for the fun of it, saying that she didn't like the way Emma rolled her eyes.

Nowadays, children think they can call 911 on you. That's all upside down. When I was coming up, the adults had the right to discipline the children. Even Ms. Beda, when I think back on it, she performed a valuable service. She was the watch lady. Every neighborhood should have one. She had no children of her own, so she would keep a watch on all of the neighborhood children. And I really think she kept us safer. There was a big road near where we lived, Pine Street. For our own safety we were forbidden from crossing that road. But we always wanted to cross it because there was a good play area on the other side. We'd start walking toward it, but when we saw Ms. Beda on her porch, then we'd turn around and come back. We'd know she was standing there just so she could keep an eye on us.

As the situation with Uncle Rufus became more and more desperate, Emma sought the shelter of Aunt Sally's as often as she could. But eventually Uncle Rufus found a way behind her defenses.

He began wooing Jessie.

Uncle Rufus was an attractive man, popular with girls. He usually had an adult girlfriend — in fact, he had three children of his own, by two different women in Durham. He dressed well, and he knew how to present himself. It was not hard for him to charm a naive girl like Jessie. Rufus mounted a charm campaign against Jessie even as he continued to abuse Emma.

Emma had watched with alarm the developing friendship between her pedophile uncle and her nine-year-old girlfriend. Several times, she came home from an errand to find Jessie and Rufus sitting together on the porch. Often, Jessie was sitting right in Uncle Rufus's lap.

I wanted to warn her, but I didn't know how. She seemed just so taken with him. I didn't know how she and I could be looking at the same man and feeling so different.

For a long time Emma felt too ashamed and embarrassed to confide in her friend. But one day, when they were both sitting in the bath together at Aunt Sally's house, their conversation turned to their bodies and the different feelings they had. Jessie was a year older than Emma, and Emma could sense a curiosity and excitement in her friend that was far from how she herself felt. Unwilling to let go of the moment of confidence between friends, Emma poured out the truth about her Uncle Rufus and the things that he did to her.

There was a pause while Emma's story sank in. They were expecting Aunt Sally to come in at any moment and start scrubbing them. Emma was terrified that the revelation would disgust her friend, perhaps make her not want to see Emma again. But a part of her also hoped that Jessie would jump to her defense. Perhaps she would even tell Aunt Sally and help save Emma from the abuse. At the very least she wanted her friend to be warned.

But nothing prepared her for the sparkle that she saw creep into her friend's eyes.

"Whoa, girl, that should'a been me!" Jessie finally said.

Emma could hardly believe her ears. "But Jessie," she said, "It's *doing the nasty*—it ain't no game."

"Yeah," breathed Jessie. "I know." Emma could see the barely restrained excitement in her face.

Their conversation in the bath had the exact opposite effect from what Emma had intended. Jessie began visiting Emma's house more often than ever. And Emma began to suspect that Jessie was actually looking for times when she knew Emma would be away. When Emma came home, her heart would sink as she saw her best friend cuddling and laughing with the man whom she saw as the embodiment of evil.

Before long, it was clear to Emma that Jessie had fallen in love with Uncle Rufus.

> *She was only nine years old. She didn't even have no breasts. And yet I've seen him kiss her there, just as though she was a grown-up lover. I felt that the more she let him do, the more he'd be getting into practice, and use it on me. He'd give her money, buy stuff for her. And she seemed to just love him more and more. She thought he could do no wrong.*

Eventually, Jessie began having sex with Uncle Rufus. Unlike Emma, Jessie's relationship with him was consensual—as much as a nine-year-old can consent. As she heard her friend talking about her unnatural relationship with Uncle Rufus, Emma began to feel that instead of being her best friend, Jessie was someone whom she had to get away from.

In some ways I thought of it as a betrayal. She knew what he'd done to me and how I felt, and still she'd tell me how he was handsome and she was crazy about him. When I heard her say that I just didn't want to be around her so much.

Jessie was not the only friend of Emma's who fell into her pedophile uncle's clutches. Jackie was older than Emma, a friend who was more like an older sister. After Emma became distanced from her former best friend, she and Jackie became closer. And Emma told Jackie about her abuse at the hands of Uncle Rufus. On one occasion, Jackie came to stay with Emma. The girls knew that Anna was going to be out drinking, and they felt that two of them together would be able to resist Uncle Rufus better than Emma alone.

Late that night, after the two girls had fallen asleep in Emma's bed, the door opened and Uncle Rufus crept into the room. Emma woke up to the familiar suffocating terror of her uncle's weight on her bed. Crying out in terror, she woke her friend lying next to her.

Jackie tried to help Emma struggle against her uncle. But he was not to be put off so easily. In fact, the presence of another girl in his victim's bed seemed to excite him to bolder action.

Rufus leered at Emma's friend, his breath heavy with liquor. "Well now, I might leave her alone if I can have you instead," he said.

At twelve, Jackie was old enough to understand what Uncle Rufus was demanding of her. Uncle Rufus's vulture hands lifted off his battered niece to light on the soft skin of this new, fresh prey. For what seemed a long age, Emma lay frozen on her side listening to her uncle grunting and thrusting and her friend quietly whimpering.

When it was over, Jackie lay sobbing beside her. Desperate for comfort and love, Emma took her friend in her arms, and the two girls lay together, rocking each other with pain and grief.

Now it was no longer Emma alone who was a victim. Her uncle's evil had spread to envelop her two closest friends. Emma knew that if she didn't do something, the horror of her uncle's abuse might destroy them all.

Finally, she decided to tell Aunt Sally what was happening between Jessie and Uncle Rufus. And as she saw Aunt Sally's eyes widen with shock at the tale she was telling, she went on to tell her of the things that Uncle Rufus had been doing to her for the past two years.

Although Aunt Sally was horrified at what she heard, it did not come completely out of the blue. Jessie was always talking to her about Uncle Rufus, and Sally had been wondering for some time how Jessie had even gotten to know him. Now it was as though the scales fell from her eyes. Jumping up, she marched straight to Anna's house to confront her about the abuse.

It was like dropping a bomb on Emma's peaceful household. Anna listened to her cousin in growing anger, humiliation, and despair. She had not been able to believe it when her own daughter tried to tell her of Rufus's depredations, but coming now from another family, she had no choice but to accept that her brother was a child molester and a rapist. Anna was a dutiful mother and a protective sister. But she was also a fighter. Once she was convinced of the evil that her brother had carried out, her anger spilled over like river in flood.

She sent Gerard out to hunt down Uncle Rufus and bring him back to face her fury. But her boyfriend returned empty-handed. Uncle Rufus had gotten word of his sister's wrath and fled to Virginia.

Jessie was furious with Emma for telling on her lover. But Emma knew she had done the right thing — and she had acted in her own defense.

I wouldn't have told, but I knew it weren't right. Sometimes you don't know when things done by adults are wrong. But with him, I knew. What he did was pure evil.

Worried about the damage and disease that Rufus might have caused her daughter, Anna took Emma to Lincoln Hospital to have her examined. It was the first time Emma had been subjected to a gynecological exam. Her childhood was ending much, much sooner than it should.

A little while later, word came that Uncle Rufus was in jail in Virginia. In spite of all her disillusionment, Anna helped get him out of his scrape just like she always had. Adding insult to injury, she leaned on Emma to write the letter for her, enclosing the money that would allow him to get out on bail. Uncle Rufus stayed away for all of the next year, but then one day Emma came home, and there he was sitting on the front porch. He did not even smile at his niece.

By now, though, Emma's tempestuous relationship with her uncle had become an open-clawed battle. Emma no longer had to hide her hatred and terror of her uncle. And in fact, she used his return as an opportunity to put into action her plot for revenge.

While he was gone, Emma had used every opportunity to prepare her attack on her uncle. She had done her best to egg on the men of the neighborhood, who were talking about teaching Uncle Rufus a real lesson if he should ever show his face in town again. Now her time had come. Going the rounds of the neighborhood men, Emma let it be known that nothing would please her more than to see her uncle get his comeuppance. The most outraged of the neighbors was Mr. Herndon, a neighborhood leader who had always disliked Uncle Rufus.

Mr. Herndon got the neighborhood men together and hashed out a plan of revenge on Emma's behalf. That night, when Uncle Rufus threaded his way down the street on his way back from one of his drinking parties, Mr. Herndon accosted him.

"We don't like perverts in this neighborhood," he said.

"What did you do to Emma?" chimed in one of his neighbors.

Soon, Uncle Rufus was surrounded by angry men. Grabbing him and throwing him to the ground, they began kicking him like a beaten dog, smashing their feet into his face and sides until he could hardly move. At last, Emma was getting her revenge.

> *That's the first time I wondered if something was wrong with me. I got so happy, such pleasure from it. I was there in front of those men, just watching it all. In a way I was embarrassed, I didn't want everyone to know what he'd done to me. But Lord, I was so happy that day! I looked at that beat-up face for days afterward, and I was so glad I didn't know what to do. Jessie cried and blamed me; that was really the end of our friendship. But I knew what was right. Rufus had it coming.*

Just as Emma's problems with Rufus were coming to this climax, Anna's boyfriend, Gerard, began to act strangely. He would often sit drinking with Anna, but increasingly the alcohol began to affect his mental balance.

Anna loved Gerard, but her relationship with him had always been stormy. Both Anna and Gerard were fighters. Anna, who had been independent for years and who had taken Gerard into her own home, did not want to be controlled by a jealous boyfriend. Gerard on the other hand was obsessive about Anna's relations with other men.

If she just talked to a couple of men he'd go crazy. Every weekend they'd get in a fight. At bedtime, we'd decide whether or not to take off our clothes according to atmosphere. They might be having so much fun drinking in the room next door. But then we'd suddenly hear things breaking and Mama hollering. That's when we knew to be ready to leave the house with Mama in a hurry.

One night, Anna had been working the late shift and came home at midnight. Emma and the boys had been waiting up for her, getting increasingly nervous as Gerard drank in the room next door. He seemed to be brooding, boiling for a fight. Soon after Anna got home, the shouting began. The children cowered in their room while the adults screamed at each other. Then Anna came running into Emma's room and told her to grab the boys. Emma didn't need any instructions — she was ready to go. Quickly grabbing her brothers, they ran out of the house, with Gerard shouting after them. As they scurried up the street, Emma looked back and saw Gerard chasing after them. Terrified, Anna ran to Fayetteville Street and took her children into the only place that was open, a fast-food restaurant called the Chicken Box. The restaurant was owned by Peggy and Claiborne Tapp, a husband and wife who were friends of Anna's.

Breathlessly, Anna told Peggy to call the police. Tap came out and tried to calm Anna down. "I'll talk to Gerard," he said.

But when Gerard burst into the restaurant he grabbed Anna and started violently struggling with her. In the struggle he tore her dress from top to bottom. Anna, infuriated, suddenly produced a knife. In another moment she had slashed at Gerard, cutting him about the chest, arms and throat. The blood started oozing out, and the fighting stopped as suddenly as it had started. Anna stood there with a bloody knife, and everyone took in what had happened. Claiborne dialed 911, and when the police car arrived, he found an old cardboard box to put on the seat of the cruiser to prevent Gerard from bleeding all over it. The last Emma saw, Gerard and Anna were being driven away by the police, Gerard to the hospital and her mother to jail.

But even then, Anna's relationship with Gerard staggered on for a little longer. He recovered from his wounds and went straight to the jail to get Anna released. Gerard refused to testify against Anna, so the charges against her were dropped. And somehow the two of them patched up their relationship.

The fact is, my Mama loved Gerard. We all loved him. It's just a shame that he began acting so strange. We wondered if it was because he had fallen off the back of a truck one time that he had a nervous breakdown.

The relationship finally ended when Gerard began experiencing hallucinations. What had been a low-level problem of depression and introspection flared into out-and-out delusional mania. One time, he was convinced that the house was being attacked by wild Indians. Anna had to call the police to restrain him. Soon after, Gerard left their house to go back to Wilmington.

The Chicken Box restaurant. The scene of a dramatic incident in which Emma's mother stabbed her lover. Established in 1957, the fast-food restaurant on Fayetteville Street is still operating today (North Carolina Collection, Durham County Library).

My Mama cared a lot about Gerard. It was a hard decision to send him away. I was sorry too. He would have made a good dad. I know her heart had to break at some point when she made these decisions. I know she asked herself, "Am I going to be able to take care of my children if things don't work out?" But she made the decision that had to be made. And she never gave up her financial independence; she never leaned too much on a man or anyone else. She had a lot of common sense to compensate for her illiteracy.

In 1962, Emma started at Whitted Junior High, a pioneer school founded by African Americans in the 1880s as North Carolina's first African American grade school. Her best friend at her new school was Lucille. The two were so close, many people thought they were sisters — and Emma and Lucille encouraged them to think so. After school, Emma would sometimes be allowed to go hang out with her friend. In those days, much of the entertainment for the black community was centered on Pettigrew Street. A favorite haunt was the Regal movie theater.

One day, after watching a movie together, an older girl approached them. "I've been seeing you around," she said. "Why don't you come and hang out with us?" She was with a group of boys and girls, all older than Emma and Lucille. Emma had to say no — her mother imposed a strict curfew on her. But Lucille's family was more permissive, and she went to join the older group later that evening.

All that week, Lucille could talk about nothing but these new friends she had made. Because they were older, they were more exciting than the middle school kids the girls normally spent their time with. The following weekend, Emma told her mother that she was going to the movies, but instead she and Lucille went to meet their new friends. At the center of the group were David Hitchens and his twin brother Dan.

It felt good to be included with them. They were all a little older. They knew things. They smoked; some drank — they just seemed like the coolest people. They told us they'd been watching us. They knew we'd go to the movies — the meeting wasn't by accident. That made me feel special. So anytime I could slip away, I'd always go where they were.

Their main haunts were liquor houses and Ben's store, where there was a "piccolo" (jukebox) for the young people to play and dance. Emma

Regal Theater and Biltmore Hotel. The Biltmore Hotel was the pride of Durham's Hayti district. Built around 1929, the hotel was one of the preeminent hotels catering to African Americans in the Southeast. For Emma, though, the neighboring Regal Theater was the main attraction. All of Durham's movie theaters were segregated, and the Regal was at the heart of black Durham's lively entertainment district (© Durham Morning Herald Co. Reprinted with permission).

and Lucille were accomplished dancers — they had learned in the schoolyard to dance to the music of the Temptations, Gladys Knight, the Miracles, and the Chi-lites.

> *Lucille and I could dance real well. That intrigued them more.*
> *She and I would swing together. We taught them how to swing. It*
> *was a lot of fun. At first, I just loved to hang out with them—I felt*
> *popular. But after a while, I realized that I was infatuated with*
> *David. When he showed me attention, I accepted it. I thought it was*
> *cool to be with a twin—they looked just the same. You'd have to get*
> *real up on them, or ask them: which are you?*

At first, Emma thought that her new friends were just a little older than her — surely if they wanted to hang out with a couple of middle school girls, they couldn't be so much older. But David and Dan turned out to be much older than Emma — already in their twenties. Rather than scaring her off, David's age added to his appeal. Emma hardly recognized the danger she was putting herself in.

I had no business in that adult world, but I thought I was being cute. I came from a secure home, so I had no street smarts. Before I met David, I'd never have consented to have sex with a man. But he really was my god. I just loved him to death. People say children can't fall in love, but I think they can, and I did. I was so infatuated with this man that I'd have walked on coals for him. Whatever he said, I'd just love to hear him talk to me.

And so, not long after her thirteenth birthday, she began sleeping with David. In spite of her strong feelings for him, she was reluctant at first. She'd had very little formal sex education, but after her experiences with Uncle Rufus she had a feeling of distaste for anything connected to sex. And she knew perfectly well how her mother would feel about her having a sexual relationship with a grown man. But in the end, her passion for David overcame all her scruples.

It wasn't an often thing. He had to talk me into it every time, because it hurt every time we did it — and I also hated that I was hurting my mother.

In spite of her worries, her new, adult relationship had her walking on air. But she began running into the complications of adult affairs almost immediately.

First, she had to deal with her lover's infidelity.

David was very popular with girls. He was of below-average height, but he had clear, dark skin and a beautiful, deep voice that made people love to hear him talk. It wasn't long before Emma began to realize that she was not the only girl in his life.

Even worse, her main rival turned out to be her own best friend. Lucille had fallen for David just as heavily as Emma had. David played the two girls off each other, and in the end, he caused them to fall out and their friendship was destroyed.

Lucille's family was less strict than Emma's, so she was able to go out freely while Emma had to stay home. One day, while Emma was stuck at home, a mutual friend of theirs, Esther, came to her house and told her that Lucille was "going" with David. When Emma refused to believe it, Esther told her that she could go and see for herself: the two of them were together at that very moment, in Ben's store.

"Everyone hangs at Ben's," said Emma.

"Well, Miss Lady, I'll let you see for yourself."

Anna had already gone to sleep, so Emma slipped out of the house and she and Esther walked over to Ben's.

No one saw us. I was just standing at the entrance to Ben's looking in. And there they were. He was sitting in a chair, and she was in his lap, his arms around her. Oh, how that hurt! It hurt for what he had done to me, but even more for her, because I loved her like a sister. Now we could never be the same again!

Emma cried for days. Even her mother, who was not normally sympathetic about Emma's emotional life and who highly disapproved of David, felt bad for her.

Even after she had confronted him over his own infidelity, David remained fiercely jealous and possessive of Emma. Sometime after the revelation of David's infidelity with Lucille, Emma went alone to the movie theater. While she was there, she bumped into a classmate — a boy — and after the movie he offered to walk her home.

We were walking, and playing and hitting each other. We were just kids, for goodness' sake. I don't know where David came from, but suddenly he was there in front of us.

"Got you a new boyfriend, have you? Y'all just couldn't quit giggling. I was watching you."

Next thing I knew he had knocked me down, and then he jumped on that boy. Hurt him too. He was lucky; he could have been jailed — where I come from, you had to do something really bad to end up in jail. But this came close.

After this first outburst, David began hitting Emma regularly. It didn't matter that he was cheating on her; if she did anything he considered inappropriate for "his" girlfriend, he hit her. Even when she again caught him making out with her former friend Lucille, his reaction was to become abusive. Emma had no one to confide these sorrows to — in fact, she had to hide her bruises at times to prevent her mother from getting suspicious.

And then Emma realized that she was pregnant.

Chapter 2

Learning the Hard Way

Emma had only a vague understanding of the facts of life, and if she had suspicions about her changing body, she had done her best to suppress them and live in denial. It wasn't until the fourth month of her pregnancy that the changes became so obvious she could no longer deny them.

It was her home economics teacher who forced her to acknowledge it. In the second semester of her eighth-grade year, the curriculum included sewing classes. The assignment was to make a dress, and when the teacher helped Emma take her measurements, she immediately realized that Emma's proportions were not those of a normal thirteen-year-old. The teacher took Emma to the principal, who, following the school's policy, suspended her from classes until she could present a doctor's certificate that she was not pregnant.

Her school's policy was to deny attendance to pregnant girls. At the time, this policy was justified as an attempt to ensure that pregnant girls received at least a minimum of medical supervision — and indeed, it was the first time that Emma was confronted with the necessity of caring for her body in its new condition. But Emma saw it as punishment.

I loved school. I always did well in my classes — my grades were always As and Bs. I loved school, not just because I loved school, but also because I loved to teach my mother, who'd never had the chance to go to school. But I'd got mixed up with the wrong person. They didn't have classes for pregnant girls. They told me I was a "bad influence." Getting pregnant took away the thing I enjoyed the most. I loved school, and it took all of it away.

Emma continued to live in denial for a while longer. She continued to set off for school in the mornings, but as soon as she was sure her mother had left for her factory job, Emma turned around and came

53

home. She spent the day sitting listlessly at home, and in the evening she had to invent stories about her day at school for the benefit of her mother.

She knew that the pretense could not last. It was only a matter of time before the truant officer came calling. The officer showed Anna a letter from the principal, urging Emma to visit a doctor to get herself checked up. Anna couldn't read the letter herself, but she forced Emma to spell it out to her. When Emma read the section about her suspicious measurements, her mother went pale.

"Measurements?"

She pulled my clothes tighter to see the outline, and she could tell immediately. I thought I was going to get a whupping, but instead my mother burst into tears. She started wailing and going on. She did whup me later, but that crying hurt worse than any licking she could ever give me. I'd have let her whup me all day and all night. I had never wanted to put no tears in my Mama's eyes. She was the Queen Mary as far as I was concerned. I broke my mother's heart. I was the only girl she had, and she expected more from me than that.

Although Emma's family attended the African Methodist Episcopal church in their community, Emma's parents were both Catholics. Probably Anna had converted to Catholicism when she married Kingfish. In this crisis, she turned to the priest of the Immaculate Conception Catholic Church. Immaculate Conception ministered to a mixed-race congregation, and its priest was a white man. Anna needed his support not only because he was a minister and her family was in crisis, but also for very practical reasons: Anna could not read or write the registration documents for her daughter, and she needed an educated person to help her. No doubt Anna turned to him also because he was outside her community and would not contribute to the gossip that was sure to circulate. If that was the plan, it backfired. The priest offered to come with Emma and her mother to the hospital to support them in their crisis.

I was the only person standing up in the maternity section of the Lincoln Hospital with her Mama and a priest! Everyone was looking at this little black girl and her black Mama and this white priest, registering to see if she can get a pregnancy test. The priest had to

explain everything to my Mama and then he had to fill in her
responses on the paperwork, so I was standing out there with him
and Mama for a long time. People were coming and going all around
us, and I knew some of them. They saw me with the white priest,
and they were saying that I must have got pregnant by the priest!
And of course it got back to David before I could even tell him.

Emma had no desire to bring David back into the picture. She had
not got over the hurt of his betrayal, and she had resigned herself to
losing him to her best friend Lucille. But when David learned she was
carrying his child, he came back to her — for a while at least. However,
her boyfriend's return just set Emma up for more heartbreak. It was only
a matter of time before she caught him being unfaithful again. The situation was complicated. Lucille by this time had a new boyfriend, and
in fact she was pregnant by her new lover and had been suspended from
school shortly after Emma. But David continued to vacillate between
the two girls. Emma was no longer surprised, but that did nothing to
soften the hurt.

He'd betrayed my trust one time, so I was looking. But I'll tell
you, I didn't want to find anything. The more I stayed with him, the
more I cared for him. It was terrible to be pregnant and to see your
boyfriend going with your best friend.

In the end it was David's mother, a powerful woman called Ms.
Gwendolyn, who intervened to protect Emma. Ms. Gwendolyn took
responsibility for Emma's medical care, escorting her to the hospital for
check-ups, every two weeks at first, then — because Emma was considered
high risk due to her youth — every week.

Emma had little idea what to expect at the culmination of her pregnancy, and when she began feeling abdominal pains just a month after
her fourteenth birthday she wanted to believe it was nothing more than
a stomachache.

I'd been staying active throughout my pregnancy, playing with my
friends and feeling completely healthy. So I wasn't prepared for any-
thing unusual to happen.

For the first few hours, the pain came and went, but during the
course of the following day, while Anna was at work, Emma's pain got

worse. It had begun to feel like the worst stomachache of her life. When Anna got home she immediately saw that something was wrong, but like Emma she did not immediately make the connection with Emma's advanced pregnancy. Instead, she gave Emma a couple of aspirin to help reduce the pain. Soon, though, the cramps were coming strong and fast, and Anna realized that she needed to take her daughter to the hospital.

They went to Lincoln Hospital, and Emma was immediately admitted to the maternity ward. Her labor was by this time very far advanced, and almost immediately the doctor ordered for her to be prepared for delivery.

> *They wanted to put my legs up in the stirrups. But I wouldn't let them do that. It was more than I could stand. I was in this room with bright lights shining down on me. And I had no idea what was going on. My Mama wasn't allowed in the room. I asked one of the nurses what was happening, but instead of answering me, she said, "If you hadn't done what you done, you wouldn't be here." One of the other nurses stood up for me. She said, "She's asking questions. She wants to know what's happening. Give her a break." I was in pain, I was crying, and more than anything I wanted my Mama. I was calling for her. But the first nurse said, "You didn't call your Mama when you were doing what you did."*

Thankfully, Emma's labor didn't last for long — she had already endured most of it at home. In a very short time, she delivered a healthy baby girl.

After she was wheeled from the delivery room back into the maternity ward, Emma was allowed to see her mother. And soon after, the little baby was brought out to join her.

The nurse tried to show Emma how to breast-feed her daughter. But neither she nor her mother had any intention of keeping that up. Before the birth, she had stocked up on baby bottles, condensed milk, and Karo brand corn syrup.

> *No one told me that you needed to keep breast-feeding. So when I got home, we had the bottles ready. My Mama showed me how to prepare them, and that was what we gave to my baby.*

When she stopped breast-feeding, Emma felt her breasts swell and then become hard and painful. Anna's remedy was to rub ointment on them, then take a rag and bind them tightly, fastening it with safety pins.

She changed that cloth every other day. And as she did so, my breasts got smaller again and they didn't hurt anymore. Sometimes the old-school remedies really work!

Emma fell in love with her daughter from the moment she set eyes on her.

I just loved Donna to death. She was the most beautiful baby I'd ever seen. It wasn't just me that thought that. Other people said so too. I loved to keep her clean. I changed her diapers even more than I needed to. She smelled so good. I can still remember that smell!

Meanwhile, Donna's father had learned of her birth.

David visited the hospital. He brought the baby some things. But he didn't come to see me. He just left some stuff for the baby. My Mama and Ms. Gwendolyn didn't even tell me the stuff was from him. They knew I wouldn't want to use it. Of course, he had to act good. He owed me. He was lucky — my mother could have put him in jail. A grown man going with a thirteen-year-old girl was certainly against the law. But I didn't even know you could get into trouble for that.

There was never any question that Emma would be the one to take care of her baby. Her mother taught her the basics of child care (Emma also attended prenatal and postnatal classes at Lincoln Hospital), but Anna was fully occupied with her job, and she had her own life to live. Emma's school would not accept a young mother as a student — her school days were over. She spent her days at home with Donna, changing diapers and playing with her daughter.

But she still had to deal with her Uncle Rufus, who after a period in jail in Virginia had returned to his sister's house. Anna had been horribly wounded by her brother's betrayal of her trust, but she also recognized how much Rufus depended on her. She was the only mother he had ever known. And so, when he had nowhere else to go, she allowed him to take up his perch once again.

After Rufus was beaten up by the neighborhood men, his sexual attacks on Emma had ended, but even now he continued to behave hatefully to her. Between her abusive and unfaithful lover and her abusive and perverted uncle, Emma had no male figure in her life to model what a good husband and father might be able to offer. She was to suffer throughout her life from this vicious cycle of abusive relationships.

Most hurtful of all to Emma was her mother's disappointment. Her relationship with her mother, who was the one fixed star in her troubled life, could never be quite the same again. When she looked at her daughter, it was no longer with the same sparkle of happiness and trust. That said, in some ways the incident deepened their relationship. Anna herself felt partly responsible for Emma's plight, and her innocent joy in her daughter was replaced by a new, loving protectiveness. In fact, Emma's experience was by no means unique. Several of her classmates had dropped out of school because of pregnancy — in fact, they formed a small community of friends for Emma, with the shared experience of young motherhood and exile from school.

With the new baby's arrival, Anna's house was full to bursting. Her sister Mary was still living with her on and off, sleeping with Emma and Donna on a rollaway bed; and Uncle Rufus was sleeping on a rollaway in the boys' room. And now Anna brought yet another person into the household: a boyfriend who lived with her until his death in 1969.

His name was Frank Spruce. Frank had come to Durham from South Carolina, and he made his living working odd jobs in construction. He was severely epileptic, and his disability prevented him from ever working a steady job. But he made enough to pay his keep, and he soon became a treasured member of the household.

> We all loved Frank. He was a quiet man, and he was gentle. But he was funny. He could just make you laugh about anything. He'd be sitting on the porch a lot of the time, and he'd say to you, "Come here." And you'd go over and pretty soon he'd have you laughing until you were crying.

At least once or twice a month Frank would have a seizure, and Emma's family members — whoever was nearby — would rush to put a spoon in his mouth to prevent him from biting through his tongue.

Frank made his own condition worse by his frequent drinking bouts. Everyone knew that the liquor wasn't doing him any good, but he lived in an environment where everyone drank — Anna was herself a heavy drinker, and Frank's mother Ms. Leetha made her living selling illegal liquor.

Ms. Leetha thought the sun rose and set on Frank, so she wasn't going to go criticizing him. Even I tried to talk to him sometimes, but it wasn't any use.

In a world in which fights and domestic violence were a common occurrence, Frank was a gentle figure who avoided a fight whenever he could.

No matter what my Mama said to him he never hit her. I never saw him but once strike my Mama, and that was more like a reflex — it happened so fast, and it was because she had done something hurtful to him. Usually he would just walk away. He would go out and sit quietly on the porch, and he'd wait for her to come out and talk it through with him. Or he'd wait till she had gone to sleep; then he'd come back in and lie next to her.

At home with the baby, Emma was thrown very much on the company of Ms. Gwendolyn, who turned out to be a doting grandmother. Although her sons were eventually to father many children by different mothers, Donna was Ms. Gwendolyn's first grandchild, and she loved her all the more for the difficult circumstances of her birth. She often invited Emma and the baby over, and Emma could count on her to babysit when needed.

Ms. Gwendolyn was a remarkable woman, one of those powerful, self-sufficient women who continued to form the backbone of African American society in the inner cities. She ran a vigorous business out of three houses that she owned in the center of black Durham, together with her business partner Fred Gaines. All of the houses operated as illegal drinking places. They served liquor to working men and women who might stop in for a drink at any time of the day or night. In addition to a variety of conventional liquors — bourbon being the most popular — they also sold homemade "white lightning," which many people swore was superior to any brand-name liquor. The white lightning was distilled by specialists and distributed on the black market by illegal traders — people like Emma's father. Some liquor houses also sold an evil-looking brown liquid called "home brew" that was said to be made with banana peel among other ingredients. The houses contained piccolos, so they functioned as dance halls as well as bars. Mr. Fred also ran a gambling business: on game days, he would set up a table and sell tickets offering bets on the winners of professional ball games. Emma still remembers the winners shouting, "I've got a hit!" as they watched the games on television while drinking in Ms. Gwendolyn's houses.

Ms. Gwendolyn's houses also doubled as boarding houses. She rented out the bedrooms to single men, who would eat her traditional southern meals of fried chicken, greens, beans, and rice. In fact, so popular was her cooking that many men who roomed in other houses came to her for meals — she would charge them a weekly rate, payable after they received their wages on Friday.

Anna insisted that Emma's first duty was to take care of her children. That meant feeding them, washing their cloth diapers at the kitchen spigot, nursing them when they were sick, and tending to all their needs.

> *It was all hand wash. And those diapers, they better be white! My Mama wouldn't let you put no off-white diapers out on the line. I use Clorox to this day — it was my savior! And you didn't bring those diapers back in the house without folding them nicely too. And you better have done all of your caring for the baby if you want to go out to a movie.*

The arrival of baby Donna was an added expense for Anna, and Emma worried about the financial burden she was causing for her mother. And so she kept her eye open for work opportunities. She thought she had found one when she saw a flyer for a nurse's assistant position at the John Umstead mental hospital. Emma applied and got the job, and for several months she took the bus at 6:30 every morning out to Butner, a thirty-minute drive from Durham, leaving baby Donna in the care of Grandmama May or Ms. Gwendolyn. Unfortunately, though, her job came to an abrupt end when she was attacked by a patient.

> *He got mad at me because he didn't want to take a bath. He just "amped out" on me. I ran, but he ran after me. They keep all the*

60

doors locked in there, and I knew I could never get my keys out in time. Well, you could tell the Lord was working that day. It just happened that as I arrived at the door with him right on my tail, one of the nurses had just unlocked it. So I zipped out. Only he zipped out too. I ran to the doctors' office, and he chased me in there. I quit that same day!

It was the only full-time job Emma has ever held.

Emma had been heartbroken at David's betrayal of her in favor of her own friend, Lucille. But after Donna's birth, David seemed to be genuinely smitten with his first child, and he showed a sincere desire to be reunited with Emma. Emma was still only fourteen, so there was no question of marriage — although David said he would like to marry her if he could. But for a while, Emma allowed herself to believe that Donna had brought her and the man she loved back together.

And she did love David. Of that there was no doubt. It was because she loved him that it had hurt so much to see him drifting away from her. Now she seemed to have him back. For several months, David visited Emma and his daughter at her mother's house. He brought presents for Donna and he paid more attention to Emma than he had in a long time.

But it wasn't long before he resumed his pattern of betrayal, violence and abuse. The endless cycle of jealousy between Emma and her friend Lucille continued, and so did the beatings and outbursts of violent anger.

I don't know why black men seem to have the gumption just to beat on their women. They just seem to think it's a natural thing to do.

Once again Emma realized that for her own survival, she had to break off the relationship. And once again, David did not make it easy for her. The violence and betrayal that characterized her relationship with David were cruel lessons for a fourteen-year-old mother to learn. But an even harsher experience awaited the child who just months earlier had been a happy young schoolgirl.

It was Christmas. After her breakup with David, Emma felt free to entertain new admirers. One of the most fervent was David's own twin brother, Dan. On the last working day before Christmas of 1964, Dan came over to deliver an early Christmas gift for Emma. It was a beautiful red sweater. Emma was thrilled with the present, but she was also busy. She had to take care of Donna, and she also wanted to clean up the house. Anna was coming home early that day for the Christmas holidays, and Emma wanted the house to look spic-and-span when she walked through the door.

Finding it hard to get Emma's attention, Dan sat for a while with Uncle Rufus, who as usual was home stirring up trouble. Soon, the two men were drinking together. Emma hated to see them together, even more so because as fast as she cleaned up, Uncle Rufus and Dan would mess up the living room with cigarette ends and dirty glasses. They were drinking Thunderbird wine — cheap, strong, and rough. Dan was not a drinker. It was as though Uncle Rufus was deliberately getting him drunk.

There was nothing uncommon in Emma and Uncle Rufus exchanging sharp words. She did not try and hide her hatred of the man who had poisoned her childhood. And she was furious with him for sitting with her friend messing up the house while she was trying to get things nice for her mother's return. Nor was there anything unusual about Uncle Rufus answering back. The exchange of insults and hate-filled words was a daily part of their routine.

But it was a new departure when Uncle Rufus pulled out a gun and started waving it wildly in Emma's direction.

Stupid with drink, Uncle Rufus allowed all of his pent-up venom to come out. Waving the gun at Emma, he poured out a torrent of abuse and filth. Seeing the gun, Emma froze in terror. She had come to believe that her uncle was capable of any act of violence, even murder. She knew that he hated her for the shame and beating he had suffered two years earlier. Uncle Rufus himself had taught her what it meant to hate.

In the small house, there was nowhere to escape except the front door. But surely her uncle wouldn't really dare to use a lethal weapon in his own sister's house. A moment later, a tremendous explosion filled the room and rang out into the neighborhood. The shot tore into the floor beside Emma's feet and sent her running to the door. But in her terrified state she could not get the door open. It was swollen with the winter humidity, and when she pulled on it the door would not budge. Trembling with fear, Emma crouched down on the floor.

Uncle Rufus sat on the sofa laughing at the mayhem he had caused.

"Here," he said to Emma's friend. "It's your turn. Did you see how she jumped? I want you to make her dance for me!"

Dan was in love with Emma. He had come to the house to bring her a Christmas gift. He had no reason to participate in her torture. But Uncle Rufus had gotten him so drunk that he had taken leave of his own wits.

Taking the gun from Rufus, Dan began waving it wildly in the air, laughing like a madman.

Terrified beyond rational thought, Emma clawed at the front door of the house, desperate to open it and tumble out, but unable to move from her position hugging the floor. Just as Dan squeezed the trigger, the door swung open and Anna walked into the house. Instantly, amid the deafening roar of the handgun, she collapsed onto the balcony rail. The bullet had hit her squarely in the stomach.

The chaos that followed was beyond description. Anna sagged bleeding and groaning on the porch, while Dan stared with disbelief and horror at the consequences of his act. Emma rushed to call the emergency services, and soon the house filled with paramedics and police officers. Dan was placed under arrest, and Anna was transported to the hospital.

It took months for Anna to recover from her injury, and in many ways her life came to an end at the moment the gun exploded in Dan's hand. Her recovery was slow and extremely painful, and she never went back to her job at American Tobacco. She was recovering in the Duke hospital when she slipped and fell trying to climb up into her bed, and her wound reopened and spilled her intestines out into her hand. Rushed back to the emergency room, she had to undergo more surgery and more weeks in the hospital.

When Anna did at last come home from the hospital, she had no hesitation in passing final sentence. Rufus was never again to be allowed in her house. Dan was sent to prison, but he would have got a much longer sentence had Anna not pleaded for him from her hospital bed. She was in no doubt who was to blame.

Emma's life has in many ways been dominated by her bitter feelings toward her abusive uncle, and the destructive path that her life took in response to the abuse.

All my life I've picked abusive men. I had sense enough to get away from them in time, but still, I picked them. And all my life I've had a mistrusting—it's been so hard for me to give my heart in trust. And there's more. Because of my experiences, I've made myself be strong. Even when I was married, I had to show strength. That can be a problem too, you know, when you don't want to look at the other person's point of view. If you just can't step back and let your husband take the lead, that can be a problem. You take it away from your man. That steals his manhood. When you care so much about somebody—that can be a real problem. In a sense, I learned to be an abuser myself. All of that comes from my experiences being abused as a little girl.

Could she have done more to stop the abuse before it became too entrenched in her life?

Today, I'm sure that man would have been locked up. But back then, people didn't trust the police. The families in my community, their first loyalty was to each other. We were taught, "You protect your family." So we didn't go running to the authorities when we had a problem.

Emma did carry out one small act of revenge. After the shooting, Uncle Rufus made himself scarce once again. He knew well enough where the blame lay for the harm done to his sister. Uncle Rufus had left behind a drawerful of the fine clothes that he loved to parade himself in, and one day Emma and Junebug carried his clothes out into the yard, poured gasoline over them, and set them alight.

I was so happy to watch that man's things go up in flames. Lord, you don't know how happy that made me. It was wrong of me, I know. But sometimes the evil in others will bring out the evil in you.

Emma turned fifteen in July 1965. She was still a child in most senses of the word; but even if the scars of her uncle's crimes were invisible on the surface, the baby she carried with her around the neighborhood was a marker of her sexual experience. For many men, she was an inviting target: a young girl, still with the magical fragrance of childhood, but experienced and available. The men from Emma's neighborhood, men who had known her since her infancy, continued to treat her with respect and consideration. But Emma attracted the attention of several outsiders and newcomers, some of them much older than she was. As experienced as Emma had become in life's dark lessons, she had little time for the innocent boys of her own age. She looked to men for strength and protection. And she found herself fatally drawn to the very men who most resembled her early abusers.

Richard Austin was thirty-two years old. A construction worker who had moved to Durham from South Carolina, he lived in the next street over from Emma's with his wife and two small children. His brother Frankie was also living with him. Initially Emma got to know Frankie. But even though Frankie showed an interest in Emma, it was Richard that she was attracted to. Emma assumed though that Richard was unavailable. No matter what the chemistry, she drew the line at having an affair with a married man.

But not long after they met, Richard's wife left their home, returning to South Carolina with the children. And Richard told Emma that he had never been married to her in the first place. Now that his woman was gone, Richard pursued Emma urgently. He told her that she was the only girl he had ever loved. He told her that he wanted to marry her. To an impressionable fifteen-year-old girl, his pursuit was irresistible.

Richard's courtship of Emma was not all smooth, however. One day Emma answered a knock on her front door to find Richard's former girlfriend — the mother of his children — on the porch. Taking in Emma's childish frame and the baby in her arms, she said, "I've come to take Richard back. He belongs to me and his children. He has responsibilities."

But Emma was no longer an innocent little girl. She had learned to fight. It was one lesson that the harsh events of her childhood had taught her well. "Richard is mine," she retorted. "You're not married to him. You don't have any claim on him."

Her defiance was strengthened by the knowledge that she was pregnant with Richard's baby.

Late in 1965, Emma moved out of her mother's house and began living with Richard in his house on Crest Street. It did not feel like such a big step. Emma still stayed often at her mother's house, which was just around the corner. But in early 1966, Richard and Emma submitted to blood tests in Durham, then took the results and traveled down to a small town outside Charleston, South Carolina. They stayed with a friend of Richard's, and two days later they were married. The ceremony was the simplest possible. No one was present except for the newlyweds and Richard's friend, who acted as their witness. Emma wore a plain beige dress and a pair of new pumps. The trip to South Carolina was necessary because in North Carolina their marriage would have been illegal. Emma was still fifteen years old.

Anna had given Emma no encouragement in her wedding plans.

My mother liked Richard, but she did not want me to be married to him. She saw things that I could not see. She saw how jealous he was. I couldn't go to the store or even to Mama's house — he would come and get me and bring me home. If one of my male friends showed up, there'd be no end of trouble. Unlike Richard, I had grown up in Durham. I knew people. But he wouldn't let me see my own friends. He wouldn't even let me see my girlfriends. He thought they were going to entice me to go out, and he didn't want me to go out unless he took me. And if he did take me out, it was a problem if I saw my own friends. But I couldn't help being known — it's where I was from! So in the end I preferred not to go out. I guess Mama could see all that better than I could. I thought I was in love with him, and that overrode all the other stuff.

Emma quickly found her new home to be a prison. Richard kept her locked up much of the time, and he would beat her at least once a week.

He'd lock me in all day long, while he and Frankie went out to work. There was mesh on the windows, and he'd lock the door from the outside and take the keys.

Emma had been used to a life of considerable freedom. Although since Donna's birth she had had to stay home to take care of her baby, at night after Anna came home, Emma would often leave Donna with her mother or Ms. Gwendolyn and go dancing with her friends. Emma loved to dance, and she was at her happiest in the small basement dance halls with their jukeboxes and illegal liquor. Once Richard came into her life, however, she had to watch her every step.

He would get very annoyed if I slipped off. As he stayed in Durham he got to know the layout of the Hayti community, and when he couldn't find me he'd come looking from one dance house to another. I got so I could tell if he showed up even if my back was to the door. My friends would stop talking and get a look on their faces. Sometimes I tried to hide before he saw me, but it usually didn't work.

Richard made no effort to control his anger at seeing Emma dancing with her friends. Often, he would hit her on the spot.

He was punch crazy. He'd hit me right in the face—blacked both my eyes sometimes. He'd hit me both with his knuckles and with the flat of his hand. He had a vein in his forehead that would start beating.

On one of the worst occasions, Richard actually broke Emma's arm.

This time, it was me that was jealous. Richard and I had gone to a liquor house near our home. It was a place he loved to go to. He liked to gamble—he was real good at it—and this place had gambling as well as dancing and liquor. They also had food—fried fish and chicken. Usually I didn't like going with him to this place. He wouldn't let me dance, so what did he expect me to do while he gambled? I would feel feisty, but I wouldn't be able to let out my feelings. Well, on this night I went into one of the rooms and saw him in a corner with my school friend Catherine. And it wasn't just chitchat they were having. I could see that it was serious. Frankie had told me that Richard had a thing for Catherine, so I was already on my guard. Well, when I saw that, I got real mad, and so I went into the next room where there was music, and I began dancing with my friends. At first I was dancing with my girlfriends, Lucille and Shirley. But that night there was a boy there who could dance so well. And he saw me dancing, and he asked me to dance with him. And I thought, well, if Richard is sitting there in that corner with Catherine, then why shouldn't I? And we were really good together. We were so good that the people were standing around us in a circle, watching us dance. Then suddenly Richard was there, dragging me out from that circle. He took me by the arm and began twisting it. I thought maybe he was just showing off his power over me. Once we got out in the street he loosed my arm, and instead he crooked me by the head. By the time we got home I was spoiling for a fight. I was so mad! I accused him of cheating on me with Catherine, and he took my arm and twisted it again. And this time he twisted it so hard that it broke. Frankie came in and saw what had happened and he called an ambulance. The police came too, and they arrested Richard. It was the only time he went to jail. But they let him off with a fine.

Richard's violent behavior was not only directed at Emma. He carried a knife with him at all times, and he would not hesitate to use it.

He didn't have to cut anyone — it was hard to get anyone to go up against him. He wasn't afraid to use fists or a weapon.

On one occasion, Richard turned on a harmless young man who worked in the Peter Pan, Emma's local grocery store.

Bob had a speech problem. He could hardly talk. Well, on this occasion I had stopped to talk with Bob. I had no idea that Richard had followed me. There was absolutely nothing intimate between me and Bob. In fact, I could hardly understand a word that he said. But when I turned around, Richard was there. He pushed me to the ground, and then he turned on that poor boy. Bob hadn't done no harm to anybody.

Richard had not settled down to life in Durham. He kept talking about moving. He wanted to go to New York, where he felt that there would be new opportunities and new horizons. He would talk to Emma with shining eyes about the big city life, free of the old constraints of southern racism. Emma wanted to believe in him, but in her heart of hearts she knew that she was not going to leave Durham.

As abusive as he was showing himself to be, I knew that if I didn't have my Mama and brothers around, I'd be in terrible trouble. And besides, there was no way I was going to go so far from Mama. I had the sense not to follow him.

In the final months of 1966, Richard's restlessness grew into a firm resolution. He decided to leave Durham before the end of the year. By

68

this time he understood that Emma was not going to go with him. Perhaps he too had seen the other side of his fairy-tale marriage to a child bride. It was as though they had both been living in a dream.

Soon after Richard's departure, Emma gave birth to a second child: a son, Jake.

> *After Jake was born, Richard came back from New York to see us. I guess he had missed us, because this time he thought he could make me and Jake go with him. It was a scary time. I stayed incognito as much as I could. I was worried that he would force me to go to New York. But somehow I managed to stay out of his way. He came to visit several more times after that. Once he even got into an altercation with my then boyfriend. But then one day, about a year after he left, I got some papers in the mail. He had filed for divorce in New York. I signed the papers and that was that.*

In the closing months of 1962, the city of Durham had asked voters to approve a bond issue for the demolition of the entire district known as Hayti — the district where Emma had been born and lived all her life, and where more than 50 percent of the black population of Durham lived.

The idea for a program of "urban renewal" had emerged as part of a national campaign to reverse "blight" and renovate downtown areas, which were becoming increasingly threatened by the growth of suburban residential and retail development. A federal report said, "Our cities are caught in a descending spiral which leads to widespread municipal insolvency. The accumulated and continuing spread of blight eats away at the assessable base of the cities. As the blight spreads, it is inevitably followed by crime, fire, disease, and delinquency."

"The city's middle-income residents are fleeing to the suburbs," echoed Durham's conservative, white-run *Durham Herald* newspaper. "Modern shopping centers are drawing business away from the outmoded downtown business district with its congested traffic and parking snarls. The city keeps upping the tax rate, because a large part of the tax base is deteriorating as slums and residential blight spread through the town. An apathetic public shrugs it off as the common course of events.... Slums, once on 'the wrong side of the tracks,' grow to envelop all but the main street."[1]

The city's elites could bring powerful statistics to support their indictment of Durham's inner-city residential districts. [2] Industrial employment in Durham had fallen by 20 percent since the end of the war, factory workers' wages were stagnant, and the downtown infrastructure was becoming increasingly dilapidated. The median income for families in Hayti was only $2,100 a year, less than half the city average. Sixty-five percent of residents had less than a fifth-grade education. Fifty-five percent of the housing units were considered unsound or lacking in plumbing facilities, and 30 percent were overcrowded. Diseases of all kinds were more prevalent than elsewhere. Venereal disease in particular was rampant, with more than one hundred new cases being reported a year among a population of 6,500. Hayti was also the worst district in the city for infant mortality, illegitimate births, and arrests for crime.

A journalist from the *Durham Herald* put these statistics into words and vivid images. He described his visit to the black neighborhoods of Hayti in the tones of an explorer venturing into exotic and unknown territory. Leaving the city of orderly streets and well-appointed housing, he entered a run-down maze in which the poorly engineered roads allowed water "to form small lakes with sticks, boxes, rusty cans and pieces of clothing floating about." He described the ramshackle houses: "Few families could boast of windows throughout their homes; banisters swayed haphazardly on some porches, rooftops showed years of wear with tin and assorted shingle patches; rusty window screens hung lopsided; and rotting steps sagged and dipped from want of replacement. Adding to the general dilapidated state were junked cars scattered here and there, grass from at least two summers growing around them; cast-off appliances on porches and in backyards, their innards ripped out by children for toys; trash heaps, coal piles and stacks of wood within reach of back porches; and broken bottles, cans, old mattresses and an assortment of other debris thrown up under the houses." These conditions "are conducive to ill health, transmission of disease, infant mortality, juvenile delinquency and crime." The area "has only about 11 percent of the city's population. Yet, it is the scene of 21 percent of the pedestrian traffic accidents, 20 percent of the tuberculosis cases, 23 percent of the infant mortality, 15 percent of the major crimes, 20 percent of the juvenile delinquency, 41 percent of the venereal disease cases, and 20 percent of

This page and page 72: Hayti neighborhoods, 1958. White journalists advocating the destruction of Hayti saw conditions "conducive to ill health, transmission of disease, infant mortality, juvenile delinquency and crime," but for Emma these streets represented security and pride in her strong community (© Durham Morning Herald Co. Reprinted with permission).

71

the illegitimate births." Given these grim statistics and the general air of irredeemable hopelessness in the area, there could be only one conclusion: "Those living in these areas, in 90 percent of the cases, will greatly benefit from the relocation program."

The city commissioned a team of students at UNC's School of City and Regional Planning to study how Durham might best take advantage of a new federal program to assist in "urban renewal"—a program that offered federal funding for two-thirds of the cost of approved projects. The students presented a plan for the complete reconstruction of the Hayti area. The city created the Durham Redevelopment Commission to draw up detailed plans and submit the paperwork to the state and federal governments. The plan was enthusiastically supported by both the black and white elites, who not only saw the prospect of a revitalization of the inner-city area, but who also no doubt were attracted to the prospect of quick profits on the purchase and sale of the affected land.

A public hearing was held on September 4, 1962, to discuss the proposal to raze the entire Hayti district. Only 65 people attended, many of them not residents of the affected area. One white woman asked "if the commission was not treating the symptoms instead of the disease. She contended that the people make the homes, not that the homes make the people."

The next day, an editorial outlined the case for proceeding with the project. "Durham can't expect sound city growth from this rotten core. The blight of the Hayti–Kay Street renewal area discourages everything but the shabbiest sort of development within its limits. It destroys values in adjoining neighborhoods until they too become slums.... The area obviously absorbs more and more public services even as it contributes less and less value to the city. It is a social and economic drain that affects us all ... an area which takes much and produces little or nothing of value." The $8.6 million bond issue to finance the Hayti renewal as well as a slew of other reconstruction projects passed with a low voter turnout and a slim three percent majority.

And so the bulldozers began pushing into the neighborhoods of Hayti, and the families living in their path were served their eviction notices. The city promised that the displaced families would be given

73

Urban renewal, Hayti district. Within months, a flourishing community was turned into a wasteland. Evicted residents were moved into housing projects, while many of the demolished neighborhoods remain bare and forbidding to this day (© Durham Morning Herald Co. Reprinted with permission).

equivalent or better accommodation as part of the resettlement plan, but it wasn't able to deliver on its promise. There were only two public housing projects in the city, and one of them was reserved for whites. The "Negro" housing project, McDougald Terrace, was already full, with a waiting list of qualified families ready to move in. The city was working hard to expand McDougald Terrace, but the new apartments were not yet ready. In the meantime, most families were thrown onto their own resources to find alternative accommodation.

Anna had been living in her house on Spence Street for more than twenty years. But now the writing was on the wall: soon their neighborhood would be pulled down. In 1966, shortly after the departure of her husband Richard and the birth of her second child, Emma and her entire family — Emma's children Donna and Jake, Anna and her boyfriend Frank, and Emma's brothers Lionel and Junebug — moved from the house in which Emma had grown up to a new address on East Darnley Street.

It was not a big change. Darnley was adjacent to Spence, so they stayed close to their neighbors. The house was similar in age and amenities. But the move was the first in a series of adjustments — some in response to city initiatives, some in response to family circumstances — that would eventually move the entire family into the all-black housing projects. If Hayti was a slum, Emma was never aware of it. She saw instead the vibrant neighborhoods, the close friendships, the mutual support, and the dynamic local economy, both legal and underground. She felt a deep sense of belonging that has never left her.

> *The community I grew up in was well taken care of, even though I now realize we were considered low income. There was a community of hardworking, proud people that took pride in the upkeep of the neighborhood. We children had to help inside and out. Where you come from does not define who you are or will be — and that was the attitude of the community.*

At sixteen, Emma found herself in a new home, crowded together with six other family members as well as frequent long-term visitors. She had no job, and little prospect of bettering herself or of improving her prospects. But that did not stop her from dreaming. Emma dreamed that one day she would be able to complete her education. She dreamed that she would be able to use her considerable academic talents to pursue a worthwhile career. But in the meantime she struggled with the daily responsibilities of caring for two small children. Emma, scarcely more than a child herself, felt the burden of her premature motherhood as she boiled diapers and watched over her babies while her heart longed to be out studying, working, and playing with her former classmates.

And then a possibility arose that seemed to open the way for Emma to get back on the track to improving her life and prospects.

At first, the arrangement seemed ideal. Jackie was one of Emma's closest and dearest friends. Their friendship had been cemented forever by Jackie's protection of Emma against the depredation of Uncle Rufus. By now, Jackie was married to a gentle and much-liked man, Reggie. Jackie and her husband Reggie led a stable, relatively prosperous life. They both had high school diplomas, and they both had steady jobs —

Reggie working in a nursing home for the elderly, and Jackie as a janitor in the hospital.

Jackie was high spirited and full of fun. She was a large woman, and her ample figure always attracted men, especially older men.

> She had a way of walking, sticking out her chest and butt. She had a big butt like her Mama. I don't know how white folks feel, but black men like big butts. And she used it. We benefited too. Her admirers were always doing little things for us. One of them, Oscar, was a taxi driver. And even if Jackie wasn't with us, we'd call him from wherever we happened to be, and Oscar would come and pick us up. Of course, he never charged us.

But Jackie and Reggie carried a hidden sadness. Jackie's doctor had told her that she could never have children. Seeing Emma with two children that she could barely manage to take care of, Jackie suggested one day that she should take in Donna and adopt her.

> I knew that Jackie was really in love with my daughter. I knew that both of them loved children. And they both had good jobs. I felt they could give her so much more than I could.

And so Emma agreed to sign the adoption papers, and Donna moved to Jackie's family with the new last name of Lafontaine. Although it was hard for Emma to lose her daughter, she was comforted to think that Donna was living with a safe and loving family. Jackie and Reggie both adored their adopted daughter, and between them they offered both financial and emotional security.

Not long after parting with Donna, Emma also gave up baby Jake. But unlike her decision to give up Donna, Emma's parting with Jake was unintended and bitter. Emma became, in fact, a victim of what she still thinks was a conspiracy between two of her best friends.

Katherine Wright was sixteen years older than Emma — in Emma's society, that made her old enough to be Emma's mother. They had met on the dance floor — several of Katherine's younger relatives frequented the same dancing houses as Emma. Soon after their meeting, Katherine began to take a strong interest in Emma. In fact, they became almost inseparable.

Katherine was much older; it never even gave me pause to wonder why she found me so friend-worthy. Katherine was like a big sister, even a mother. She felt safe.

To Emma, one of the most appealing aspects of her friendship with Katherine was the freedom that she enjoyed in her friend's home. Katherine was good company, and she encouraged Emma to drink and smoke at her house — habits that the teenage Emma still did not dare practice in front of her disapproving mother.

Soon, Emma and baby Jake were spending more of their time at Katherine's house than at Anna's. Katherine encouraged Emma to feel at home. If Jake got sleepy, Katherine made a place for him to lie down. If he soiled his clothes, Katherine washed them for him. She encouraged Emma to leave some spares in her house, and as Emma got more comfortable with the arrangement, Katherine even went out and bought Jake new clothes, toys, and baby items. She made no secret of the fact that she adored Jake, and Emma was pleased and flattered by the attention her friend gave to her baby son.

Katherine had a son of her own, Junior. Junior was just a year or two younger than Emma, and once they got to know each other better, Katherine told Emma that she thought it would be perfect if Emma and Junior would become a couple. She said it was her fondest hope that her son and her dear young friend should one day get married and have a family of their own — and that she would thereby become Jake's grandmother. Emma thought of Junior as a younger brother. She had no romantic interest in him at all. But she did not want to hurt her friend, so she just laughed and shrugged her shoulders when Katherine brought the subject up.

Meanwhile, Katherine began taking an interest in Emma's education. She thought it was a shame that someone as bright and capable as Emma had been forced to quit school in the eighth grade. Katherine had heard that the Social Service Department was going to offer classes leading to the GED certificate, and she promised to arrange for Emma to attend these classes. She offered to take care of Jake while Emma was in class. Emma jumped at Katherine's suggestion, and her gratitude to her older friend grew even more.

In fact, the classes never happened. Perhaps it was harder to organize than Katherine had thought; perhaps Katherine had never intended for Emma to go to class. Meanwhile, Emma got so much into the habit of letting Katherine take care of Jake that she actually came to think of Katherine as a second grandmother to her child.

And that was exactly what Katherine wanted.

As the classes that Katherine had promised receded ever more into the distance, Emma began to wonder why Katherine insisted on spending so much time with Jake. Emma began to think that perhaps she should take more responsibility for her own son and not allow her friend to carry so much of the burden. And slowly she began to get suspicious of Katherine.

Emma began hearing rumors. Katherine was known to be fond of small children, and Emma learned of an incident in which Katherine had previously tried to take custody of the children of a relative. And Katherine was not popular in the neighborhood. She lived on the same street as Emma, up on the corner of Pine Street. Emma's godmother Aunt Eve, who kept a store on Pine, had known Katherine all her life, and she warned Emma several times: "You've got to watch that woman." But at first Emma was too excited at the thought of going back to school to heed her godmother's warning or her own suspicions.

I thought she just naturally loved children. I had no way of knowing that she had already tried to take over two children in her own family.

Katherine seemed to be taking good care of Jake, and indeed she lavished him with toys and presents. Moreover, she refused to take any payment. Perhaps this more than anything else should have alerted Emma to the possibility of trouble down the road.

Finally, Katherine told Emma that she planned to keep Jake and rear him herself.

She said that if I was going to get Jake back, then she would make me pay for every penny that she had spent on him. That included all the nice things she had bought for him, even though I never asked her to buy any of those things. And I was still a minor, and she knew that. She said that she'd hired a lawyer, and if I wouldn't give her the money she'd go after my Mama and make her pay it. I don't know if she really had a lawyer or not, but I was young and I believed her. It was one thing for me to fight against her, but I wasn't going to drag my Mama into it.

Feeling bewildered, betrayed, and frightened, Emma gave in to her supposed friend's demands. She reasoned to herself that Jake was already as comfortable with Katherine as he was with Emma. Emma told herself that Katherine loved Jake, that she would look after him and perhaps give him opportunities that Emma herself could not. And she consoled herself that so long as she went along with Katherine's wishes, she would always be able to visit her son. The one thing she refused was to sign adoption papers that would permanently relinquish her rights to Jake's custody. She continued to hold out hope that one day Jake would come back to her.

But as she raised Jake, Katherine had ample opportunity to imprint her own view of the world on his developing mind. She brought him up believing that she was his real grandmother. And while she never denied that Emma was Jake's mother, she followed her own fantasy and made Jake believe that Katherine's son Junior was his biological father. And of course Jake believed her and came to love Junior as a father. As Jake grew older, he began to resent Emma—first for insisting that the man he thought was his father was not, and then, once he accepted Emma's story, for abandoning him. To this day, Jake feels resentful that Emma allowed him to be brought up by someone else even while she held on to her younger children.

And not long after the disaster with Jake, things began to go wrong for Donna too.

Shortly after taking in Donna, Jackie unexpectedly became pregnant with her own baby. One of the reasons she had taken Donna was because she was convinced she could not get pregnant. The adoption papers had been signed and there was no question of giving Donna back, but inevitably Donna had to accept a new status in the household — a status that in some eyes was inferior to Jackie and Reggie's natural-born son.

Then, a few months after the birth of their child, Donna's adopted father Reggie was killed.

Reggie's death was a mystery that left his wife — and Emma — suspicious for the rest of their days. It happened one night when Reggie went out drinking in the woods with some friends of his from work. Reggie worked in a nursing home for the elderly, and he had been shocked at the mistreatment he witnessed of many of the residents. Not one to keep his concerns to himself, Reggie had accused several of his coworkers of abuse. On this night, for reasons that have never been explained, Reggie got out of the car he was riding in and began walking, even though it was late at night and they were out in the country. Had he had an argument with his coworkers? In any case, shortly afterward the same car he had been riding in struck him down and killed him.

> *I think it's mighty funny for some "friends" to go out together, and one of them ends up hitting and killing another. Everyone was really wondering about that. The driver was a coworker. They were supposed to be friends. But they could never explain to Jackie why he was out there walking — walking to a club way out in the boondocks.*

The police treated Reggie's death as an accident, and it was never fully investigated. This was the first time, but by no means the last, that Emma felt that a possible crime against a black man was not treated the same way as a crime against a white man.

Reggie's death and the birth of Jackie's son changed the chemistry of Donna's new family. On one hand, their material circumstances improved. Jackie received compensation for Reggie's death — whether from the insurance company or from the man who killed him, Emma never found out — and eventually she was able to buy a house of her own and live a reasonably comfortable life. But still, Jackie was devastated by her husband's death, and her friends held her up the only way they knew how — with alcohol. That was hardly likely to improve her care of her adopted daughter.

But the thing that changed most for Donna was the new prominence in her life of Jackie's mother, Ms. Sally.

> *Ms. Sally wasn't a little strange; she was a lot strange.*

Ms. Sally was notorious for beating children. They didn't have to be her own. Any child she considered fair game, and she took inordinate pleasure in choosing from her collection of switches and canes.

She would whup you with ironing cords, switches, whatever she could get her hands on. Sometimes Ms. Sally would whup whoever happened to be in the vicinity.

Emma had known Ms. Sally all her life and she was used to her foibles. But Donna was a helpless victim in her clutches. With Jackie so distracted from her duties as a parent, Ms. Sally increasingly became a presence in Donna's life. In addition to Ms. Sally's innate propensity to beat children for no good reason, she also had a disturbing prejudice that made Donna's position even more precarious.

I didn't know it till later, but Ms. Sally was color conscious. She had one light-skinned daughter, while Jackie was brown. She wasn't half as dark as me, in fact, but Ms. Sally didn't like Jackie so much, nor did she like Jackie's children—her son Reggie, and my daughter Donna. Jackie's brother Jasper and sister Joyce were light skinned, and she always favored them. Anything Joyce did wrong was always someone else's fault.

Donna was a dark-skinned child, and for this and other reasons she became a particular victim of Ms. Sally, from whom she had no escape. Ms. Sally beat her repeatedly and mercilessly, leaving scars on her back that she bears to this day.

If I had known she had this thing about dark-skinnedness, or that Donna would have to spend so much time with her, I might not have let things go the way they did. Jackie didn't like it. But Jackie was attached to her Mama. I was used to Ms. Sally too. But I wouldn't have chosen to let her babysit my child.

Even more worrying than Ms. Sally was the change in Jackie's own attitude. Although Jackie was a close friend of Emma's, she was even closer to Emma's nemesis, Katherine. Perhaps under Katherine's influence, Jackie began preventing Emma from visiting with her daughter. Jackie said it was because of her concern that Donna might grow up confused about who her "real" mother was. But Emma knew she had been listening to poisoned advice. In retrospect, Emma believes that her supposed friends Jackie and Katherine entered into a conspiracy from the very beginning to take Emma's children away from her. In the end, Emma's visits were cut off altogether. Jackie moved out of town, to a large house in the country, and Emma did not see her daughter for the next eight or more years.

> *I fought against it. My brothers went over there to check up on things. But she called the police on them. It got real messy for a while. Then some years later she came back and told me she had been wrong. But in the meantime she has favored her son, and her mother has mistreated Donna. I can't help thinking that if I had known all this would happen, I could have got my daughter back and she wouldn't have had to go through all of that. Donna missed out on her wonderful grandma. She didn't get to spend time with her like her brothers and sisters did.*

Emma kept up with Donna's progress through a mutual friend, Donald. Donald was a much older man, a deacon in St. Mark's Church, where both Emma and Jackie worshipped. But his behavior was very human. He had an affair with Jackie while she was still married to Reggie, and even after the affair was over (Jackie eventually got remarried), he remained her friend. Even more remarkable, he remained friendly with Ms. Sally, who always had a soft spot for him. Donald kept Emma informed about her daughter, and Donna herself came to see him as a close friend, an uncle whom she knew she could call on in an emergency.

Some months after the departure of her husband Richard, Emma met James Pierson.

Emma was still only seventeen years old, and men from the neighborhood continued to be attracted to her youth and energy. Perhaps they also recognized her own attraction to older men. James was a neighbor, an only child who lived with his grandmother, known to the neighborhood children as Ms. Maggie. James worked in painting and construction. His mother lived in another part of town, but she often came to stay. She took an immediate dislike to Emma, and Emma returned the feeling. But James was a different matter. Although Emma did not have strong feelings for him, he was a convenient prop after the breakup of her short-lived marriage. And before long, Emma found that she was pregnant again.

> *James was not a person I can say I was in love with. He was a person to help take my mind off Richard. After I got pregnant I real-*

ized I was not only not in love with him; I didn't even like him that well. I didn't want him around me a lot. Now that I think back on it I can see that I used him. He was my diversion from thinking about Richard.

Emma tried to break off her relationship with James, but he was not to be put off so easily. In early 1968 Emma gave birth to a third child, a son whom she named Laurence. James thought the birth of his son gave him a right to Emma's affection. He began calling on her and the baby at all times of the day and night.

What he did would be called stalking today. Everywhere I went he would turn up. It got to be like I was in a cage.

As had happened several times before, she found a way out in the person of yet another strong, older man.

Anthony Williams had just returned to Durham after serving several years in the military, including two tours of duty in Vietnam. Emma met him when he passed by her house on Darnley Street looking for Emma's godmother, Aunt Eve. Emma was sitting out on her front porch with her friend Linda-Sue.

Anthony was a tall man, and you could tell he was in good shape. He had big muscles. But I wasn't attracted by his physical appearance. Actually, I wasn't in the least bit interested in him at the time.

Emma was a little suspicious of this stranger looking for her godmother, so before giving him directions she left him out on the porch to chat with Linda-Sue while she ran inside to call Aunt Eve. When Aunt Eve said that she knew him, Emma went back out to give Anthony the directions. Meanwhile, Anthony had been making friends with Linda-Sue, and he invited both girls to accompany him up to Aunt Eve's house. Linda-Sue was happy to go with him. Emma, however, had to stay home to take care of her baby. Before he left, though, Anthony took some time to play with baby Laurence.

Anthony clearly found something attractive in Emma, and before long he began visiting her regularly.

At first he seemed to be such a nice person. But he was the same man, just with a different name. He had to go to jail for me to get rid of him.

Anthony was a fighter — perhaps that was why Emma, who was so much in need of protection and security, was drawn to him. But she soon became a victim herself. Anthony was among the worst in a string of violent men in Emma's life.

His violent and irrational behavior was worsened by his difficulty recovering from the effects of his combat experience.

> *Anthony had just got out of the military, and I think he was a bit shell-shocked. Actually he was a whole lot shell-shocked.*

One time he had killed a sniper in Vietnam. The sniper was a woman, and she had been perched in a tree picking off Anthony's comrades. Eventually Anthony located her and shot her out of her perch. When she fell dead to the ground he saw that she was heavily pregnant.

> *Soon after I began going with Anthony I became pregnant yet again. And I think my pregnancy set off that shell-shock. He'd go to sleep sitting in front of the TV, and then he'd go into one of those dreams. The next I knew he'd have his hands around my neck. He thought I was this pregnant woman that he'd shot. Mama thought he was going to kill me. Once she actually called the police. And when they arrived, he thought they were the Viet Cong, and it was all they could do to get him calmed down.*

Nevertheless, Emma looked to Anthony for protection and companionship. Her relationship with him was ambiguous. After her experience with Richard, she refused at first to move in with Anthony. But she allowed him to contribute to her financial support, and early in her nineteenth year, she gave birth to his daughter, Tamara.

Soon after Tamara's birth, Anthony and Emma moved into a house together.

The circumstances of their move were dramatic. Anthony and Emma were in her mother's house with Anna's boyfriend Frank while Anna was out at work. Anna had asked Emma to watch Frank closely, because he had been having epileptic seizures since the previous evening. During the course of the day, Frank had several more seizures, some of them following almost immediately from the previous one. Emma was used to these attacks, and she knew what to do. Getting Anthony to help her, she forced a spoon in Frank's mouth, and she laid him on his side.

After the seizures ended, Frank felt very weak. Emma offered him food, but he said he couldn't eat. He asked for some water, and then she sat with him while he went to sleep.

After Frank went to sleep, Emma played cards in the living room with Anthony. Every so often she went into her mother's bedroom to check up on Frank. He seemed to be sleeping peacefully. Finally Anna came home from her long day at the factory. As usual, she went into her bedroom to strip off her factory clothes, then she ran a bath to wash the tobacco dust from her skin. It wasn't until after her bath that Anna took a closer look at her sleeping boyfriend. Emma heard an exclamation coming from the bedroom, then Anna came running back into the living room crying, "Emma, Frank's dead."

Emma was sure that her mother was mistaken. She had just left him sleeping an hour or two earlier. But when she went into the bedroom to look, she saw that her mother was right. Frank had suffered another seizure and died. Horrified, Emma ran out of the house, desperate to go anywhere rather than stay in that house with a dead man. Anthony ran after her and forcibly brought her back.

I stayed one more night in that house, but then I went to stay with a friend. And after that I never could live in that house again.

Emma, Anthony, little Laurence, and baby Tamara moved into a small, pink house on Robert Street. By this time Emma had a small income from the U.S. government's Aid to Families with Dependent Children program. Anthony received a disability pension from the government after his service in Vietnam, and he brought in more money from his business activities. Between them, they had enough for a comfortable life, with Anthony the major income producer. But although Emma accepted housekeeping money from Anthony, she insisted on paying the rent for the house out of her own income. Throughout her life, Emma has been adamant about a principle that she learned from her mother: always be responsible for your own livelihood.

My Mama always taught me not to let no man pay your bills. To this day I still have some of that in me. Anthony would give me money, but that had nothing to do with my bills. My welfare checks would come on the first day of the month, and I'd use them to pay the bills. If Anthony gave me money, I'd buy extra. To me it wasn't about him. I had two children and I knew I had to be responsible for them. What I had been through with Jackie and Katherine really impacted me, so I was extra careful about my children's welfare.

Although Emma and Anthony did not marry, they were starting to live the life of a settled family. Emma stayed busy taking care of the children, feeding her family, washing clothes (the house had a washing machine but not a dryer — like most other mothers in the neighborhood, Emma would hang the washing out to dry in the sun), and keeping up with the other young mothers in the neighborhood.

Anthony was home a lot. Because of his pension, he did not need to hold down a job, though he had some mysterious business activities that often took him away from the house, sometimes for days at a time. But much of the time he was home.

Anthony was Emma's lover and to some extent her provider. She had invited him to share the life of her young family. But she did not welcome his presence in the house so much of the time.

Like David and Richard before him, Anthony was an extremely jealous man. He didn't like me to have company of my own — not even female company. He thought that my friends were a bad influence on me. It's true, some of my friends did outrageous things at times, but that was them, not me! But Anthony heard about their goings-on. We were a close-knit neighborhood. And so he tried to stop me from seeing them — or if they came, he'd like to be around while they were there. He thought I was too young to make my own decisions — I was only nineteen after all. But I hated him trying to control my life. It was like living with your parents!

Emma discovered how dangerous Anthony's jealousy could be when she tried to assert her freedom.

Lee was just a friend. We didn't have a relationship. But Lee had been begging for months to take me to the movies. I didn't want to let him — I knew it might be interpreted the wrong way. But one day we went, and sure enough, when we came out of the Regal Theater, there was Anthony, just waiting for us. I went over to the passenger side of Lee's car, but Anthony said, "She's not getting in that car."

Lee faced up to him and said, "I'm taking her back." He was much younger than Anthony, and he must have been scared. But he had the attitude that "I'm not going to let nobody pump me out." So Anthony pulls out a gun from his back waist band, and he says, "Take that back." And then he shoots him.

Anthony shot Lee in the thigh, then turned and left before the police and the ambulance came. Emma stayed with Lee until he was taken by the ambulance to Duke Hospital. Emma was surprised at how calm she felt.

Fighting and altercations were the norm for me. We were raised around it on a daily basis. You got so that you just accepted it.

Lee recovered from his injury, and he refused to press charges against Anthony. He remained friends with Emma, never blaming her for what had happened — though he never again asked her out on a date.

But things got worse when Emma found out that Anthony himself was carrying on with the friend who had already betrayed her more than any other — Katherine Wright.

I was too young to know just how lucky I was that he was taking his attention to someone else. But he had no intention of letting me go. And while Katherine was encouraging Anthony to cheat on me, Katherine was also cheating on her own boyfriend. At that time she was going with a very dangerous man. We were both in terrible danger with those men. But still, all I could think was how he and my friend had betrayed me.

Nor did Emma care for the men that Anthony hung out with. He would sometimes disappear with them for days at a time, and while she was relieved to have him out of the house for a while, Emma worried at times that they might be up to no good. Anthony said that he was going to Virginia to visit his relatives, but Emma didn't believe him.

Her suspicions were confirmed by her younger brother Lionel. Lionel hero-worshipped Anthony and tried to be around him as much as possible. Through Lionel, Anthony came to know several of the teenage boys in the neighborhood. Lionel was chagrined to find that some of his friends were going on "expeditions" with Anthony, while he was not invited. Eventually he confronted Anthony and asked why he never got taken along. It was then that he learned the true nature of their activities. Anthony and his accomplices were professional thieves. They were going all over Durham and the adjacent districts, breaking into houses and stealing. Now that he knew what they were up to, Lionel lost all desire to accompany them. And eventually he told Emma what was going on.

By that time I'd already had Tamara. I was in a full relationship with this man that I really did not know. He was very abusive and very strong. He'd choke me before he'd turn me loose. So I found out a lot of things in a short amount of time, his temper being one of them.

Still, nothing prepared her for the dramatic end to her relationship with Anthony. One afternoon, Emma was in the kitchen fixing something to eat for her family. Anthony had come home a little earlier. Emma had not been out to greet him. He had been in the habit lately of showing up in the company of some unsavory characters, people Emma did not want to talk to. So he had showed himself in and was somewhere in the back of the house. Little Laurence and Tamara were on the couch in the living room.

Suddenly there was a loud knocking on the door. Alarmed, Emma went to see who it was. The moment she opened the door, a man with a gun thrust a badge in her face, and a half dozen of his associates, all armed with assault weapons, forced their way into the house.

They were asking me where Anthony was. I was so terrified I literally couldn't speak. Instead I just started crying and shivering from terror. I had no idea what we were supposed to have done, but I felt as though I was going to be accused of something terrible. I thought I'd go to jail and lose my children. I'm not usually too afraid of things, but those men scared me to death. I was so frightened that I even started to wet myself.

The men pushed past Emma and marched into the back of the house. Emma heard them opening the back door, and the sound of boots as several more entered the house from the back. A moment later, they came through into the living room with Anthony bound up in handcuffs and leg irons.

"She doesn't know anything about it," he said. "Leave Emma alone. She's got nothing to do with any of it."

Emma cowered with her children beside the sofa, while the officers (they turned out to be from both the FBI and the local police) ransacked the house.

> *They were searching everywhere — behind curtains, under the beds, in the closets. They turned everything out onto the floor. I had to get the children off the couch so they could search it. They looked under it and behind it, they even tore the covers off of the pillows. I didn't even know what they thought they were going to find.*

The officers were interrogating Anthony. Anthony kept telling them that they must leave Emma alone. Finally, he told them that if they could guarantee Emma's freedom, he would show them what they were looking for. But he would not take their word for it. He demanded to be put on the phone to their senior officer, and then he asked for a written guarantee. Only when the officers had agreed to those conditions did he tell them where under the house to look. The officers raced out of the house, and Emma heard them exclaiming as they gathered next to the entrance to the crawl space.

It turned out that Anthony was keeping an arsenal of illegal guns under the house. When Emma went out to look, she saw the officers laying out row after row of weapons on the ground. Anthony was telling them exactly where to look, and as they followed his directions they kept finding more. All Emma's neighbors were gathered around, staring at the amazing sight. They had seen the agents' van but had assumed they were just coming to raid one of the illegal liquor houses that operated on the street. They were astounded that their neighbor turned out to be a gun-runner.

> *They had him under surveillance, you see. I had no idea. The police asked me if I was aware that there were guns under the house, but I'd never seen any guns before. They knew I didn't know what he was into. They confiscated all those guns, and one of the FBI men told me that I was very lucky — "You and your children were in constant danger," he said. I didn't have any idea. When he had money, I just assumed it was from his army service.*

89

Anthony was sent to the federal penitentiary on a long sentence. He and Emma had never married, so Emma was free once again.

By 1970, when she turned twenty, Emma had had a world of experience. Since the turn of the 1960s she had been repeatedly raped, then physically abused by three predatory men in succession. She had given birth to four children by four different partners, and she had lost custody of two of them because of her own limited resources. In a scene of unbelievable domestic chaos and violence, she had been shot at, and her mother had taken the bullet. Emma had tried her hand at work but seemed now destined to a lifetime on welfare. She had only a seventh-grade education. She had no work skills. The neighborhoods in which she had grown up were being torn down piecemeal. And — mostly as a defense against the abuse she suffered from Anthony — Emma was already heading down the path toward alcoholism.

> I realize now that the drinking became a crutch so that I could stand the abuse from Anthony. He was so violent that I couldn't answer back; I couldn't ever tell him what was in my mind. I didn't like the things he was saying and doing to me, but I couldn't retaliate. It's hard to walk around holding something in all the time. When you don't get it out, it just doesn't go away. Drinking became a way that I could forget it.

The one significant advance in Emma's welfare during this decade came from the development of massive federal programs initiated in response to President Lyndon Johnson's War on Poverty.[3] Throughout the 1960s, successive initiatives were created to increase economic support for America's huge underclass, and to offer essential nutritional and medical services to the needy — including the poor and unemployed, vulnerable children and their mothers, the sick, and the aged. More than six million Americans — including Emma — began receiving public assistance for the first time through the expanded welfare system. The vast majority of these were mothers claiming child benefits through the Aid to Families with Dependent Children (AFDC) program.

Parents who received AFDC funding were required to participate in public employment projects, and they could lose their benefits if they refused to enter the programs or if they refused other legitimate work opportunities. The intention was clearly to get families off the welfare rolls as soon as they could find work. A wide variety of employment and training programs were implemented to help put welfare recipients back to work. But in spite of these programs, the rise in recipients was relentless throughout the decade. Critics, indeed, blamed the AFDC program for creating a class of "entitled" mothers who benefited from giving birth to illegitimate children and who had little real incentive to go out and get jobs.

In 1964, Congress passed the Food Stamp Act, which allowed certified low-income families (most of those receiving AFDC were automatically eligible, though the receipt of food stamps would reduce the AFDC allowance) to buy food vouchers at a heavy discount to their face value. And in 1965, Congress authorized the creation of Medicare and Medicaid. Medicare provided guaranteed medical care to over twenty million older citizens, while Medicaid provided grants to states to help them provide medical services to the needy. Again, most AFDC recipients were eligible.

Also in 1965, Congress expanded existing housing subsidy programs through the Leased Housing Program amendment to the U.S. Housing Act of 1937. The expansion led to the rapid growth of public housing projects. Taken together these welfare, insurance and subsidy programs amounted to a massive increase in the safety net for poor and vulnerable families. The United States still fell far short of a full-fledged European-style welfare state, but for people like Emma, the programs offered a previously unimaginable level of security. While Emma's mother worked from the age of twelve, and continued working even when she had three small children to care for, Emma had her basic needs provided for through the welfare system.

But this federally financed underpinning to Emma's security did little to change the underlying circumstances of the black communities of central Durham, which were in many ways a showcase of poverty and need. In 1970, only a little over 20 percent of adults in the disintegrating Hayti community had graduated high school. Almost 40 percent of families with children had a single mother at their head. The majority of adults worked as unskilled laborers or in domestic service. Forty-three percent of children were living below the poverty level. Less than half the population had a regular doctor, and only a quarter had had any dental treatment or check-up in the preceding year. Less than half had any sort of health insurance. Only half were registered to vote. Child mortality was still much higher than for the population as a whole.[4] Emma's experiences were not unique or even unusual. Alcoholism, violence, family dysfunction, sexual abuse and teenage pregnancy were rife in this, the only community she had ever known.

Yet this same decade of the 1960s saw enormous strides for the wider community of Durham, both white and black. The population of the county grew by almost 20 percent during the decade, reflecting the continued draw of its vibrant industries. And the nature of those industries was changing. While in the 1940s and 1950s most migrants to Durham came to work in tobacco, textiles, or related industries, by the 1960s Durham was diversifying into a variety of knowledge-intensive industries, including medicine, pharmaceuticals, research and education. Duke University continued to grow rapidly, with its hospital becoming one of the leading centers of medical research and treatment in the South. A veterans hospital opened across the street from the Duke Hospital, adding hundreds more beds and many new jobs. Durham's higher-education offerings were expanded with the opening of Durham Industrial Education Center, later to change its name to Durham Technical Institute. And on the border with Raleigh, the Research Triangle Park opened for business on 5,500 acres of newly developed land. IBM moved into a massive new facility in 1967, and the federal government opened several major facilities on five hundred acres of land donated by the state. Burroughs Wellcome moved its global headquarters to the park in 1970, instantly becoming one of the region's major employers.[5] By 1970, almost six thousand residents of Durham had received a postgraduate education, a number that continued to grow.

For African Americans, the 1960s were an era of magnificent gains in status and opportunities. Durham had been at the forefront of the civil rights movement and of the reforms that went a long way to reversing centuries of injustice.

Civil rights had been in the air in Durham for at least two decades. Some of the earliest moves to challenge the status quo came when thousands of black northerners arrived in the area during World War II. At weekends, the soldiers flocked into Durham on special buses from nearby Camp Butner. These were men who were fighting for their country. They had no intention of abiding by the racist Jim Crow laws that were supposed to keep Durham life segregated. In one tragic incident, a black serviceman was shot and killed by a white bus driver because he had complained about being moved to the back of the bus (the driver was subsequently acquitted).

During the 1950s, a number of landmark cases highlighted the determination of Durham's black community to insist on change. In 1954, a group of four black men succeeded in forcing the University of North Carolina to allow them entry into its law school. They became the first black students at any of the white universities in the Triangle. In 1962, Duke began opening its doors to black students, first under the

Burroughs Wellcome building, Research Triangle Park. The futuristic research facility was designed by architect Paul Rudolph. It represents Durham's vision of an economy driven by science, technology and medicine (Joseph Molitor, photographer. Molitor Collection #4812, Avery Architectural and Fine Arts Library, Columbia University).

threat of legal action, but eventually with increasing willingness and cooperation.

Then, in the mid–1960s, the protests against Jim Crow spread from a few elite students to the broad middle mass of blacks in Durham. The protests focused in particular on the refusal of many restaurants to integrate. In some scenes reminiscent of the Wild West, facility owners sat in their front doors carrying shotguns and vowing to shoot the first black person that tried to enter. Some of the biggest protests were against the local Howard Johnson, which was owned by a particularly cantankerous old-style southerner who refused to even consider integration. At the peak of the protests, more than a thousand blacks and sympathetic whites joined in sit-ins outside the restaurant, leading to hundreds of arrests.

Black protest also focused on the school system, with black families increasingly challenging the segregated system and winning entry for their children into the white schools. By 1963, a half dozen black girls and boys were attending Durham High, the bastion of white privilege in the Durham Public School System.

The Civil Rights Act of 1964 brought a resounding victory to the civil rights activists. The new law explicitly prohibited racial, sexual, or ethnic discrimination in the workplace, education, and a host of other sites of Jim Crow segregation. The law unequivocally brought Jim Crow to an end in the American South.

Yet for Emma, these heady victories meant little. During the same decade that blacks made so many gains in civil society, Emma saw her neighborhood evacuated and prepared for demolition. She never had a chance to go back to school, white or black. And she was unable to raise herself even to the first rung of the ladder of economic progress and skilled work.

Chapter 3

Dreams and Realities

On July 4, 1976, Durham celebrated the American bicentennial with a three-day festival in the new West Point city park on the Eno River. The park was the crowning achievement of a growing environmental movement. The Eno, which runs to the north of the city, had been seen as nothing more than a water resource by the city's leadership. It took a concerted and lengthy campaign, led by a feisty Englishwoman, to make them change their minds and acknowledge its cultural, environmental and recreational importance. Instead of damming it as originally planned, the city bought a large chunk of land surrounding an old mill house and turned it into a city park.

The North Carolina Bicentennial Folklife Festival was a celebration of the park's opening, and of the food, music, and craft traditions of the Carolina Piedmont. It was also a tribute to the growing maturity and dynamism of Durham's increasingly diverse community.

Many of the attractions at the fair were distinctively southern. Among the most popular features were the barbecue tent, where whole pigs were roasted with traditional vinegar-laced sauces, and the folk-dance bands, playing Appalachian music to the accompaniment of shouts of "Wee-haw!" But there were also popular stalls offering Hadassah potato latkes and Greek souvlaki, and there were craft stalls featuring potters, sculptors and quilters who had moved to the area for the nurturing environment and relaxed lifestyle. The festival, which was attended by more than a hundred thousand people over its three-day run, was a celebration both of Carolina tradition and of the young, dynamic, eclectic community that Durham was becoming.

The city could showcase enormous progress over the past century. In the 1870s, Durham had been nothing but a cluster of homesteads scattered around a sleepy railway station. Now, it was one of the most dynamic manufacturing and research centers in North Carolina, a city that had seen continuous and uninterrupted growth in industry and employment and that now had a population in excess of one hundred thousand. The core industries that had driven much of Durham's early growth were now in steep decline. Tobacco was suffering from the sustained decline in smoking that began in the 1960s. The big tobacco companies had begun to diversify into unrelated industries far from Durham, and one by one the factories were closing down. The tobacco auctions had dried up too. In the 1940s there were thirteen warehouses in Durham, each taking deliveries from farmers and holding its own auction. By the turn of the 1970s there were only a few left. The last auction house, Planters on East Geer Street, was to close in 1986. The textile industry was also declining, due to a combination of outmoded manufacturing plants, rising wages, and low-labor-cost foreign competition.

But at the same time, Durham's knowledge-intensive industries were thriving. Research Triangle Park continued to expand, attracting more major corporate headquarters including Colorcraft and the General Telephone Company of the South. Duke University continued its steady growth, while Durham's historically black college, North Carolina College, became a full-fledged university and was absorbed into the University of North Carolina system. Meanwhile, Durham's cultural life was becoming increasingly diverse and sophisticated. The Durham Arts Council was created in 1975, with city funding, to promote the arts in Durham. And in 1978, the American Dance Festival moved from Connecticut to Durham, with substantial financial support from local sponsors. In the same year the Carolina Theater, which had been closed for years and at one time had been slated for demolition, raised funds for a major restoration and reopened as an arts cinema.

Yet amid all this growth and prosperity, the entire downtown area, including the neighborhoods that had once been known as Hayti, had become a ghost town inhabited only by government employees during the daylight hours, and a shifting population of vagrants.

At the heart of downtown Durham's collapse was the urban renewal project that was supposed to save it. During the 1960s, the bulldozers moved into the unpaved streets of Hayti, knocking down the flimsy frame houses and forcing thousands of families to find alternate accommodation. The gradual destruction of her neighborhood had been the backdrop to most of Emma's teen years. Behind the bulldozers came the construction crews, ready to pour millions of tons of concrete into a grand new highway.

The Durham Freeway was to connect Interstate 40 to the south with U.S. Highway 15/501 to the north. Durham received two-thirds of the funding for the highway from the federal government, and additional help from the state — all under the aegis of "urban renewal." The idea was that the freeway would anchor a rejuvenated business district that would be easy to access via the freeway ramps and that would feature a range of newly constructed office and commercial buildings in the space formerly occupied by Hayti. The planners were hoping that local entrepreneurs would jump at the chance to buy and build on the newly developed land close to the freeway, creating dynamic new commercial centers and increasing the city's tax base.

Those hopes proved to be empty. The freeway took the best part of a decade to build, and during that time the streets of downtown Durham were constantly being closed off, rerouted, and dug up, causing endless delay and frustration among users of the business district.

The black residents of Hayti had been promised great things at the time their homes were taken away from them — the city promised that they would be given equivalent or better housing in neighborhoods that the city planned to develop. But these plans were frustrated by funding shortages and poor planning. Meanwhile, the families of Hayti were forced into a variety of accommodations to their new situation, at the cost of the sense of community and security that so many of them had enjoyed.

As their homes were earmarked for demolition, many families moved into adjacent neighborhoods, often taking over houses that had been abandoned by whites fleeing the consequences of school desegregation. Soon the downtown area was surrounded on three sides by low-income neighborhoods whose residents were too poor to properly maintain the housing stock, and on the fourth by a dying factory district.

Those who had not found their own solution to the housing problem were offered accommodations in the public housing projects as space

Durham Freeway under construction. The freeway tore right through the heart of Durham's black Hayti district, leaving Emma's house the only one standing on her side of the street. Although Emma's mother lived just down the street, the nearest bridge across the freeway was almost a mile away (© Durham Morning Herald Co. Reprinted with permission).

became available, or in subsidized housing in the southeastern section of the city — neighborhoods that were already predominantly black, and which threatened in spite of the civil rights movement to perpetuate the racial segregation of the city. Civil rights leaders accused the city leadership of shunting the black families into ghettoes far from the white centers of power, ensuring that they would not vote in the predominantly white precincts and thus dilute white power.[1]

Hayti's black-owned businesses had been promised a new commercial center, which would allow them to reopen in much grander conditions than those they were giving up. Hundreds of small businesses agreed to close their doors to allow for the renewal program. Only a fraction of them ever reopened, and most of those in buildings that were little or no better than those they had left. The city built a small, tin-roofed center, promising that it was only a temporary facility, but nothing ever came along to replace it.

By the end of the urban renewal program the city had spent a total of $42 million, two-thirds of it paid by the federal government but the rest financed by city taxpayers. More than four thousand families had been relocated, as well as more than five hundred small businesses.[2] Urban renewal had destroyed a vibrant community and helped create a classic case of inner-city blight. Meanwhile, downtown businesses closed one by one as middle-class shoppers fled the chaos of the massive construction project. During the 1960s, one after another the great architectural landmarks of the downtown area fell into decay through neglect and were slated for demolition. In quick succession Durham's railway station, the Eugene Morehead and George Watts homes in the Morehead Hill neighborhood, and the mansions of Durham's tobacco and textile barons on McMannen Street were all pulled down. Finally, in 1975, the fourteen-story Washington Duke Hotel — one of the proudest symbols of downtown Durham — was demolished.[3] Shoppers meanwhile thronged to the convenience of new shopping malls in the suburbs. The land that had been Hayti remained a wasteland, and the traffic on the new freeway sped past the downtown exits toward the fast-growing suburbs beyond the city limits.

Like everyone else in her community, Emma's life was uprooted by the urban renewal project. When Emma and Anthony had moved into

WASHINGTON DUKE HOTEL, DURHAM, N. C.   107454

A postcard of the Washington Duke Hotel in its heyday, 1920s. Completed in 1925, the 16-story hotel was a landmark feature of Durham's flourishing downtown (North Carolina Collection, Durham County Library).

The Washington Duke Hotel after its demolition began in 1975. The lot, nicknamed the "Bare Square," remained empty for decades. As part of the recent downtown revitalization, a part of it was turned into a brick-paved plaza (North Carolina Collection, Durham County Library).

the little house on Robert Street, they had been close to all of the amenities of the Hayti community. But when the first section of the Freeway was built, Robert Street was cut in two. On one side of the Freeway was the community Emma had grown up in: the businesses on Pettigrew Street, the neighborhoods where many of her friends lived. On the other was a single house: Emma's.

All of a sudden, Emma's vibrant neighborhood had become lonely and frightening.

> *We could stand on one side of Darnley and look at my house on Robert. But we'd have to walk all around and under the bridge and back to get to it. People tried crossing, but some of them got hit. Crossing a freeway's not the same as crossing a little street.*

Then her mother had to move too. When her section of Darnley Street was torn down, she was moved into an apartment in the new public housing project at McDougald Terrace. Not long afterward, Emma learned that her own house would soon be slated for demolition.

They called it "urban renewal," putting in that freeway. To me, it's like they singled out the most vibrant neighborhood and businesses and then destroyed them. The Hayti area, it wasn't just housing. There were so many black-owned businesses—a newspaper, a printing shop, stores. They called it the Black Mecca. It was a self-sustaining neighborhood. We had everything that we needed—restaurants, stores, theaters like the Regal where you could watch shows, rock-and-roll concerts, gospel music. And people watched out for each other. It was rare if you were born in Hayti for people not to know who you were. We children didn't see that as necessarily a good thing. If you did something, your Mama knew about it before you even got home! But now I realize that was part of the security. We weren't afraid, all balled up like people now with murders and that. We did what we could for the people we cared about. It was like a strong tie.

I didn't know we could fight it, didn't know about anything. Having children, I just focused on what was in front of me. The awareness comes as the years go on. They promised they were going to make such a wonderful new neighborhood to replace what they tore up. They built these townhomes called Rolling Hills, but if you go and look at them now, they're all empty and boarded up. They took up-and-running places that were contributing to the community and wiped them out. I don't mean that in a bitter way, just a logical one. They changed lives; they really did. I never heard any discussion where we had a seat at the table. No one was consulted—they were just told what they had to do. That's power stripping.

Writing about it later, Emma commented,

I am the product of proud parents that came from different backgrounds, but what they did have in common was a work ethic and a desire to pay their own way. This was the general attitude of the entire community. I wonder why when urban renewal came through the city of Durham, the path destroyed everything blacks had worked so hard for and built up with everything in them so beautifully. I also wonder why no one took into consideration the devastated lives it would leave behind.

After his arrest, Anthony was incarcerated in the county jail awaiting trial. While he was there, Emma visited him twice.

> *I had to tell him what I thought. They had assured me that he was not getting out anytime soon. So I told him how I felt. He had betrayed me — he couldn't just do something honest to help me raise my kids. He'd put me in a position that I could have lost my children. He knew what I was saying was true, but even so, I think if the guard hadn't been there he would have jumped on me. He refused to acknowledge the truth of what I was saying. He felt like that I should have understood better from his point of view.*

She was on her way home from visiting Anthony when she felt a need to use the bathroom. She stopped off at Ben's. While she was in the downstairs bathroom, the whole building started shaking. Emma was sure they were in an earthquake, and she ran upstairs. But it turned out that the noise and vibration had come from a huge truck that a customer was parking in the store's garage.

> *That was how I met Jimmy Roberts. We spent some time that night listening to the jukebox at Ben's. Then I had to get home. My house was across the Durham Freeway from Ben's. I pointed to my house from over on Ben's side, and I said to Jimmy, "Do you see that little light there? I live in the only house left on that street." Jimmy said he would visit, but honestly, I never thought I'd see him again. Two weeks later, I was home alone with my children when there was a knock on the door. I don't normally open the door after dark, but this voice sounded familiar. "Someone needs to see you," he said. "Who is it?" I asked. "Just open the door." And of course it was Jimmy. "I've been looking for you for the past two weeks," he said. He had been trying to figure out how to get to that lonely little house on the other side of the freeway.*

Jimmy was a long-distance truck driver, and he was on the road so much that he didn't have a home of his own. Instead, he lived in his truck.

The more he came back to visit, the more our friendship just blossomed. And even before I fell in love with Jimmy I fell in love with the inside of that truck. It was just beautiful—it was all dark blue inside, and in the back of the seats there was a bed.

Through their courtship, Jimmy took Emma on road trips as he traveled around the country. Emma saw more of the United States during those trips than she ever has before or since. She loved sitting in the plush interior of the truck listening to music and chatting with her new lover, while the highway slowly unwound outside her window. Her children stayed home, cared for by Anna or a trusted friend. Emma felt freer than she ever had in her life.

Eventually, Jimmy found a little house on Mobile Street, and Emma moved in with him. They didn't stay there long. With so many people they knew moving out of the neighborhood, Jimmy and Emma looked at the options for living closer to Anna. Anna was in an apartment on Ridgeway Street, in the McDougald Terrace public housing project. Emma had never lived in an apartment, and she had little idea of what public housing meant. She went to see a unit that had come vacant and liked it, and soon after that she and Jimmy moved into the apartment on Wabash Street, in the same project as her mother. They began going together to Ebenezer Baptist Church on Alston Avenue. The church had become an important part of Anna's life. It would send a van around the project to pick up the attendees who didn't have cars. Anna and several of her close friends would go. Eventually, Anna joined the choir.

McDougald Terrace had been completed in 1953, one of the first public housing projects in Durham. It was developed explicitly as a black housing project. A project for low-income whites, Few Gardens, was constructed just a few months earlier.

Both projects were largely paid for with federal money. Once again, massive federal initiatives influenced the direction of Durham policy and caused it to conform to nationwide trends. Following federal directives, the city of Durham created the Durham Housing Authority in 1949, and this new institution was then eligible to apply for federal loans and subsidies. McDougald Terrace cost a total of $1.5 million for more than six hundred units. It remains the largest public housing project in Durham.

Once again, Emma insisted on renting the apartment in her own name. Her rent was calculated based on her family's income — it was capped at one-third of income. Since Jimmy was working, this came to a substantial amount, not much less than Emma had been paying for her house on Robert Street. Meanwhile, due to her family's increased income, she had lost most of her welfare benefits — all she received now was an allowance for each child under the AFDC program. Emma also received child support payments from Anthony, which he somehow managed to maintain even from prison. Even with a spending allowance from Jimmy, though, it was hard to meet the monthly bills. But the three-bedroom apartment was spacious and new, it was well equipped, and the rent included all utilities up to a usage limit.

They called it an apartment. We really didn't know what a "project" was. But now we found ourselves living in one. And as time went on, we saw the bad as well as the good side of that.

They bought furniture on the installment plan from Mr. Ward, who had a store at Five Points. The apartment was not air-conditioned, so they invested in window units. They were able to afford most of the comforts of modern life — a washing machine, a vacuum cleaner.

Well, I needed them with so many children. But God was good to me. Things come. My children have never been without food, never been put outdoors. They've seen some friends with their stuff just dumped outside. It's heartbreaking when you see it happen to someone you know. I thank the Lord that we were spared that.

Not long after, Emma and Jimmy were married at the Durham County Courthouse. Soon after, he gave up his truck and began working as a landscaper. On his own initiative, Jimmy began planting trees and shrubs along their street, as well as on neighboring Ridgeway Street, where Anna lived.

The city gave him a plaque for all of that work. Jimmy really did very good work. I've never married men that sit around.

But Jimmy, too, turned out to have a darker side to him. At first it showed itself as jealousy. Then it developed into outright abuse.

105

McDougald Terrace. The segregated housing project was built for African Americans in 1953. Many of its residents took pride in its facilities and worked hard to build the community. Emma's husband planted trees along his block on his own initiative (Simon Partner).

He felt that if you disagreed with him, you needed teaching a les-
son. He would slap you so quickly you didn't know it was coming.
After a while, I would flinch when he just moved his hand or made
a gesture. And he'd say, "What you jumping for?"

In spite of the abuse, Emma never doubted Jimmy's love for her. Their relationship was highly emotional and complex. Eventually, Jimmy's frustrated love for Emma would earn him a sentence of five years in the state penitentiary.

In 1970, Emma bore Jimmy a child, Jimmy Jr. Baby Jimmy was the apple of his father's eye. Emma had never seen her husband so gentle, so protective and nurturing. But the great joy of Jimmy's birth was soon followed by great sadness. One night, while Emma and her Jimmy were asleep in their bedroom, their baby suffocated in his crib.

There was nothing they could have done. Nobody was at fault. The doctor diagnosed sudden infant death syndrome, a misfortune that afflicts families regardless of race, class, or parenting style.

But Jimmy was distraught.

He blamed me for the death of that child. He needed someone to vent on, I understand that now. But I lost a child too! I felt at the time that I had to suffer his blame on top of the loss of my baby.

Even at the funeral, he wouldn't come in with us. I didn't see him again till late that night—he was so distraught. It took him a long time to get over it. And after it happened, his actions toward me got worse. He didn't like for me to have girlfriends, or go to the store. It was like being in prison. I always had to walk on edge, think about what was safe to say.

The following year, Emma became pregnant again, and in November 1971, she gave birth to a daughter, Brianna. At the age of twenty-one, Emma was already a mother of six children by five different men. She had been pregnant almost constantly for the past four years. Three children—Laurence, Tamara and Brianna—remained with her.

It was a lonely life. Jimmy's jealousy prevented Emma from socializing much. Instead, she stayed home with her children. Jimmy had some friends, whom he expected Emma to make friends with in turn. But they were few in number.

Jimmy did not allow a lot of people, especially men, in his house.

In spite of his evident love for her, Jimmy was a constant source of anxiety and fear, and his treatment of her drove her further and further along the path to alcoholism. She never knew when her partner might turn on her, strike her in the face, and force her down on her knees in pain and terror. As she fought against him with alcohol and passive resistance, Emma's occasionally wild behavior served only to fuel her husband's neurotic abuse. His jealousy and protectiveness drove him at times to extreme acts.

Back when we were living in Mobile Street, there was a man in our neighborhood called Mr. Sanford. He was from South Carolina. Well, this Mr. Sanford, he got drunk and called me some derogatory things one day. I was so mad that I told Jimmy. Well, Jimmy left the house and headed straight down the street toward Mr. Fuller's store.

107

That's the corner of the street that Mr. Sanford lived on. The next thing I know, they're running over to my house. "Come and get Jimmy," they were shouting.

Jimmy had taken his gun and shot Mr. Sanford in the foot.

Another time, Jimmy protected Emma's brother Lionel when *he* was involved in a shooting incident.

The fact is, Jimmy loved my family. And they loved him. I loved him. The only exception was my brother Junebug. Jimmy didn't like Junebug because he was gay.

Junebug was two years younger than Emma. Ever since he was a small child, he seemed to have been a woman born into a man's body. He liked nothing better than dressing up in his sister's clothes and playing with her dolls and it was no big surprise to Emma or her family members that when he grew up, he preferred to go with men rather than women.

Emma's brother's "difference" had always been accepted by most. In fact, the women clearly enjoyed the gay men in the community.

There was one, whom we called La Richard; he was pretty as a woman. He walked these big beautiful dogs. La Richard, he had a natural swing to his hips. He had the prettiest hair down to his shoulders. He always took great care over his appearance, and he always looked good.

Junebug's special characteristic was his voice.

Junebug had one of the most beautiful falsetto voices. Just like Diana Ross. He loved the Supremes. He and my two girlfriends would get together and sing their songs. "Oh, Baby, Baby!" They were so funny; we just laughed and laughed.

Junebug was quite open about his relationships. He had a succession of loving boyfriends, who supported him financially throughout his life — until the accident that changed him forever. During the good times, Junebug enjoyed the attentions of multiple suitors. His first boyfriend was called Butch. Butch was a handsome young man who liked both boys and girls. Eventually he got married, but Junebug kept on seeing him even after his marriage. Finally his wife got suspicious and confronted Junebug.

He said, "If you want your husband, keep him home. He was mine before he was yours."

Junebug had another lover named Rebel, who was obsessively jealous. Most Saturdays, Junebug would go to the Walltown area near the Duke campus to drink at a liquor shop owned by a friend of his. Emma was friends with the same crowd, but she stopped going with them because she came to know that Junebug's presence would always trigger a fight. One day Junebug met a man called Mac at the liquor house. As they got drunk, Junebug and Mac began flirting. Mac sat Junebug on his lap and put his arm around his neck. He began feeding Junebug drinks, putting his glass to Junebug's lips. As Rebel watched their behavior, he became more and more crazed with anger and jealousy. Finally he stormed out of the liquor house. A few minutes later, he marched back in with a gun. He pointed it directly at Junebug. Junebug leaped up and jumped straight out of the second-floor window. Somehow he landed without injury, but as he ran off into the night, he heard the sounds of gunfire behind him. By the time the police arrived, Mac was lying dead on the floor. Rebel was arrested and served a long prison sentence for the murder. By the time he was released, Junebug, too, was dead.

Jimmy, though, could not abide Junebug. He was one of the things about Emma and her family that drove Jimmy wild with anger and frustration. He seems to have been a tortured individual. Hopelessly in love with Emma, the only way he could express his feelings was through violence and anger. Meanwhile Emma's main outlets were wild behavior, alcohol, and occasional defiance.

One night, while things with Jimmy were at their worst, Emma went on a drinking binge. Jimmy, tired after his long day at work, had already gone to bed. But Emma wanted action. She knew that her friends were meeting at a liquor house, but without Jimmy she didn't have a way to get there. Although she didn't have a driver's license, the pull of the liquor was so strong that she lifted the keys from her husband's pocket and drove his car to the liquor house.

The evening turned out as wild as she had hoped. Emma stayed up all night driving from one liquor house to another, getting more and more drunk. Near daybreak, she finally decided to call it a night. She got into Jimmy's car with her friend and neighbor Shirley and began weaving her way home.

The combination of liquor and exhaustion proved too much for her. Arriving at an intersection on Fayetteville Street, she ran straight through the red light, and an instant later a car coming the other way slammed into her side. The collision threw Emma's car right up onto the lawn of an apartment building. Shaken, Emma and Shirley climbed out of the wrecked car. Both were unhurt.

It turned out that they knew the man who had hit them. Mr. Brock — better known as "One-Arm" — was a well-known figure in the neighborhood, and a friend of both Emma and Jimmy. But there was no doubt who was at fault in the wreck. When the police arrived, they arrested Emma for driving without a license and driving under the influence, and they took her straight to the county lockup.

It was the first time that Emma had to spend time in jail, but that was the least of her worries. What would Jimmy say? What would he do to her? Before the police took her away, Emma gave her wallet to Shirley and told her to go as quickly as possible to Anna, and ask her to use the money to bail Emma out.

Shirley set off on her mission, but by the time she got back to McDougald Terrace she was too drunk and exhausted to do anything but crawl into her own bed. Meanwhile, word of the accident was racing around the neighborhood, and before long Jimmy heard what had happened.

Furious, he stormed over to Shirley's house and turned her out of bed. He was so incensed that he threw Shirley down the front steps of her own apartment, leaving her shaken and badly bruised, and furious in her own right. When Jimmy left to bail his wife out of jail, Shirley called the police to file a complaint against Jimmy, accusing him of assault and robbery.

Meanwhile, Emma was waiting in the jail for her mother to come and bail her out.

They took me down and took my fingerprints and my photo. Then they told me I had to take off all of my clothes. Luckily, the lady there said that I would probably be bailed out within the hour, so in the end they let me keep my clothes and they showed me right into a cell. There were two other women in the cell. They were playing cards and they asked me if I wanted to play with them. But I told them I didn't know how. The cell was just like something you'd see on television. It had some metal bunk beds — the two girls were sitting on the lower bunk playing their game. And there was a commode and a sink, but no enclosure or partition at all. I couldn't imagine the idea of going to the bathroom with people watching me. And I asked them, "That's not really the bathroom, is it?" And they laughed and said, "Yeah, it is!" I was asking silly questions, I know, but I just had no idea what to expect or what was going to happen. They gave it to me straight, and it was hard to swallow!

When the guard came and told her that her bail had been posted, she was filled with relief. But her relief turned to horror when she saw that it was not Anna but Jimmy who was waiting for her downstairs.

When I saw Jimmy I begged them to put me back in the jail. They said they couldn't do that since I'd already posted bail. But nothing was going to make me go out there and face him. I knew only too well what he would likely do to me.

In the end Emma was able to persuade the police to let her stay in a conference room for the rest of the day. She waited until it was pitch dark before she sneaked out of the jail and called a friend to come and pick her up. Her friend gave her a ride to her mother's house. But she should have known that Jimmy would be one step ahead of her. He was waiting around the corner for her to show up.

When I looked up, there he was, running towards me. I saw the distance to my Mama's front door and I began running too. It was a near thing, but I just made it into Mama's house before he caught up with me. I slammed the door shut and locked it.

Later that night, Jimmy in turn was arrested by the police on charges of assaulting and robbing Shirley. Emma however had no intention of bailing him out. Instead, Jimmy spent the night in jail before being bailed out by some of his neighborhood friends.

After this incident, both Emma and Jimmy recognized that their relationship had reached a low point. In fact, it seemed that they could not sink any lower in their destructive embrace. But they were wrong. For Jimmy and Emma, things were still to get worse.

When it came, it was so unexpected that it took both of them by surprise. Emma had no idea how deep in her the vein of anger and resentment ran. And Jimmy — he continued to think it was his prerogative to put Emma in her place.

One day, Emma was at home preparing dinner. She was in the kitchen, cutting up a chicken. Jimmy came into the room and picked a fight with her, and before she knew it he was slapping her in the face.

> We'd been together three years. I was so tired of it. I said, "You hit me again and I'll..." And before I could say it, he did hit me again. It was like a blink of light. My brother happened to be coming through the back door at that moment. I knew Jimmy could whip Junebug. I was not going to let him beat my brother. I don't know how it happened, but I started stabbing him with that kitchen knife. Then Junebug pulled out a knife and he started cutting him too. We cut him up good. And then we ran and called the police and ambulance. They wrapped his whole head up in bandages. I knew I'd have to go to jail — I was almost as afraid of the police as I was of him. But he didn't press any charges against me.

Even this wasn't the end of their tortured relationship. Jimmy thought for a while that he had reached the end. He decided to leave her and try to start a new life. He went to live in Florida, and Emma thought she would never have to see him again.

With Jimmy away, Emma moved on with her life. It wasn't long before she began seeing another man.

> Robert came up with my brothers. I'd been knowing him for years and years. Of course, in those days I never felt anything for him except friendship — or not even that, really. I didn't like it much when he and his friends would come over. You know how brothers and sisters can be. So it was a surprise to everyone when I began dating him — my brother most of all!

Soon after she began dating him, Emma became pregnant yet again.

While Emma was pregnant with Robert's baby, the last person she wanted to see showed up at her house: her husband Jimmy.

Right away he saw that I was pregnant. It was a major shock. But he took it well. His goal was for us to get back together, so he knew not to upset me. I thought he'd be wanting a divorce, but no, he said he was coming back.

Emma was in a difficult situation. She was pregnant by one man, but the man now standing on her doorstep asking to be let back into her life was her husband. Emma felt that she owed it to her marriage commitment to give her relationship with Jimmy another chance. And in spite of everything, she did love Jimmy. Emma knew that her relationship with Robert was troubling to her husband. She stopped seeing Robert when she allowed her husband back into her life, and for a while things went smoothly as they tried to repair their marriage. But they found that they could not just return to the way things had been.

I'd been by myself a while since Jimmy left. I'd learned to be more independent. I wasn't the same person that he'd left, and we didn't know how to negotiate about what each of us needed.

Emma had developed a close network of friends while Jimmy was gone, women from the neighboring apartments in McDougald Terrace. They had in common a love for — and dependency on — alcohol. Most days, they gathered together and pooled their money for a bottle.

Everyone in my family when I came up drank. Mama too. I didn't know that drink was a drug. I had to learn as an adult about drinking being as harmful as other drugs when you're addicted to it. When you grew up seeing everyone, including your own Mama, drinking, to me it was just a natural thing. I didn't think it was the same as drugs.

They would meet most afternoons. Sometimes they'd be joined by men from the neighborhood, and before they knew it they would be having a wild party. Not content with her afternoon and evening sessions, Emma would start the day with a shot or two in the morning before breakfast. But she still managed to feed and care for her children. She describes herself as a "functioning drunk." But she did get drunk, and she did occasionally have blackouts. As she wrote years later,

For me, drinking was a way of hiding from part of my reality—
having children too young, poor education, no skills and a host of
other problems. [But] ultimately, when the alcohol is gone and the
feeling in my body is screaming for another drink, I find the problem
is still there.

Jimmy reacted violently to Emma's newly independent lifestyle. Before long, their relationship was stormier than ever, as Jimmy did his best to cut off Emma's friendships and control her behavior. And his threats and violence in turn drove Emma further to alcoholism.

Emma's baby was born in August 1973, and Emma named her after her mother: Anna. Since Emma was still legally married to Jimmy, Jimmy registered himself as the baby's father. He did his best to make sure that Robert never even saw his own daughter.

I felt bad about that. Robert didn't ask to get in the middle of that
turmoil—I thought that my husband wasn't coming back. But
Jimmy took to Anna. He had a heart for children.

Robert found a way around his rival's jealous protectiveness. He began giving money to Emma's mother, asking her to spend it on the baby. And after a while, she began letting Robert know when the baby was going to be visiting with her so he could come over and spend time with his daughter.

Around the time of Anna's first birthday, Emma's relationship with Jimmy once again deteriorated to the breaking point. After a big fight, Emma moved out of their apartment and back in with her mother. Jimmy begged Emma to come home, but she put him off, telling him that she needed some space. In a fit of emotional excess, Jimmy attacked the furniture in his own living room, tearing up all the pieces that they had saved so hard to buy. One day when Emma sneaked home after Jimmy had gone to work, she saw the devastation he had wrought. The sight of his emotional instability made her even more determined not to allow Jimmy back into her life. And Jimmy responded with an even more dramatic scene.

He promised he would replace the furniture, and in fact after two
or three days he did get new furniture. Then he came and begged me
again to go back home. I said no, not for a while, and maybe never.

Jimmy said, "You're coming home today!" And the next thing I knew, he'd gone out and fetched a bottle of Clorox, and he was holding it up in my mother's living room. "If you don't come home, I'm going to drink this bottle!" he said. I thought he was bluffing. I imagined he must have filled the bottle with water to scare me. Well, the next thing I knew, he up and drank off that bottle. Before he got halfway through it he collapsed on the floor. I didn't know what to do. I picked up the bottle and sniffed it. It was real Clorox! I said to myself, "Lord have mercy, is he crazy?" So I called the ambulance, and they took him away to the hospital. And I started wondering what crazy thing he'd do next.

Emma didn't have long to find out. Three days later, she was at home with baby Anna when a neighbor ran around to her front door and warned her that Jimmy was getting out of a cab, armed with two guns!

I looked and saw him coming, and I immediately dialed 911. I knew what Jimmy was capable of. I believed that he wouldn't hesitate to use those guns. I had my baby in the house! The police came quickly, and they questioned Jimmy and confiscated one of his guns. They didn't seem to take the incident too seriously. Probably they didn't think Jimmy would really use the gun on his own wife. I told them he had another gun, but they didn't even look for it! They just told him to go on home, and he could get his gun back on Monday.

There were five of us in my Mama's apartment that evening: me and Anna, Mama, and two friends, Martha-Kay and Ellwood. I was in the kitchen fixing a bottle for the baby when Ellwood suddenly called out, "Get down!" He was sitting by the window, and he had seen Jimmy coming with a gun. Then I heard a big boom. Anna was in the living room on the couch. Ellwood shouted not to move, but I just had to get to her. I crawled on my hands and knees into the living room. He had shot through the window, and the pellets hit the wooden part of the windowsill and sprayed the wall. There was glass and debris falling on baby Anna. She was lying hollering on the couch, and for all I knew she might have broken glass in her mouth.

I didn't care if he did shoot me. I had to do something about my child.

After Emma picked up Anna, the terrified occupants of the house ran into the only windowless room — the kitchen pantry. They waited to see if Jimmy would enter the house, but eventually they realized that he had left.

The shooting took place in the middle of a bustling housing project. Dozens of people witnessed Jimmy's attack on his mother-in-law's apartment. The police showed up soon after the incident, and later that evening they picked up Jimmy and took him away.

For Jimmy, the consequences of the shooting incident were dire. After several weeks in custody, he was tried and sentenced to five to seven years in prison. After that it was clear that there was no going back, and Emma began the process of divorcing him. But Jimmy did everything he could to prevent her, and it wasn't until 1977 that Emma was finally able to get a divorce. By that time she was back with Robert, and they had had another child, Benjamin.

It was at about this time that Emma's old nemesis, Uncle Rufus, came back into her life. After leaving her family, Uncle Rufus got a job on a construction team, working at Duke University. In 1975 he had an accident at work that left him disabled for life. Confined to a wheelchair, he was unable to take care of even his simplest needs. He went to live in a nursing home, but Emma found that she could not be rid of him so easily. Anna's health had been in a steady decline in recent years, and Emma was now Uncle Rufus's only able-bodied relative in the area, so before long Emma found that she was the designated family member for his care.

> *The nursing home, they'd ask me to come and pick him up. I guess he'd told them I was his closest kin. Well, I couldn't hardly turn him away, could I? I didn't know if it was a punishment for what I'd done or what. I'd have to change his diapers for him. But still, I kept a close watch on him when my girls were around—I didn't trust him one bit. Oh, no, he was just as mean and bad as ever. Even the night that I was laying in with Michael, about to give birth, I wouldn't go to the hospital until I'd got all the girls out of my house. I felt he*

might do anything. That was 1981— he was still torturing me in 1981! I let him come because of my Mama. In her heart of hearts, she still loved him to the end.

With Robert in her life and five children to care for, Emma was busy from morning till night. Her life was far from easy. She was often short of money, and her relationship with her partner was becoming increasingly shaky. She had noticed a change in his behavior, and she was suspicious of what might be causing it.

Then the family suffered a near disaster. One day in 1979, three-year-old Benjamin was playing alone in his mother's bedroom when he set off a fire. No one knows exactly what happened, but Emma assumes he had found a box of matches and started playing with them. Emma's neighbors saw smoke pouring out of the bedroom window and quickly raised the alarm. All the residents of the four-apartment building quickly ran out into the street — everyone, that is, except Benjamin. When Emma realized that her son was still in the building, she started screaming. The fire department had not yet arrived, but a brave neighbor ran up the steps three at a time to grab Benjamin from inside the building. He emerged a minute later, holding the unharmed child. Shortly after that the fire trucks came and put out the fire. But Emma's home was uninhabitable.

There were no vacancies in McDougald Terrace, so Emma's family was moved by the housing authority to Oxford Manor. They had lost almost all their possessions in the fire, but the Red Cross donated furniture for their new home.

They had no early prospect of returning to McDougald, so Emma and Robert did their best to put down roots in their new home. They made friends and picked up the pieces of their lives. But it was not long before Emma started seriously questioning the direction that Robert's life was taking.

Every two weeks, right after his payday, Robert had a visit from a small group of friends, always the same people. One of them was his former girlfriend, by whom he already had two children. The others were a girl called Linda and a man known as Bookie.

Right after he got paid, regular as clockwork, Robert would show up in a red car with his old girlfriend Shirley. Then Linda and

Bookie would show up. Well, I see four people, two women and two men, and they just go up and disappear into one of the upstairs bedrooms. What was I supposed to think? Of course I thought Robert and Linda were having an affair. But you know, it wasn't the affair itself that got me so mad. It was the fact that they were doing it in my house!

Emma had a friend and drinking partner nicknamed Tweetie. When Emma confided her suspicion and anger to her friend, Tweetie urged her to confront Robert. The next payday, they waited till Robert and Linda showed up in the red car.

This time I was determined to confront them. So I followed them upstairs with Tweetie behind me. As we went up the stairs, Linda was just coming out of the bathroom. I said to her, "Why can't you go to your own house? Why do you have to pick my house? Y'all must be smoking reefer! Well, I'll tell you what, it's stopping today!"

But Linda said, "No, it's not like that. We're not smoking no reefer. We're cooking up Ban." Or that's what it sounded like. It was some sort of diet pill that they'd cook up until it melted and went into a needle. Course none of them knew anything about AIDS in those days.

So Tweetie comes up behind me, and I say to her, "They're doing hard drugs!"

And when we go into that room, who do you think I see with a needle stuck into his arm? Robert!

Emma understood that her relationship with Robert could never be the same again. She warned him that if she ever found drug paraphernalia in her house, she would call the police on him.

Soon after this, Emma and Robert once again moved back to the MacDougald Terrace project. Ironically the reason was, once again, a fire.

It was a Sunday, and as always we had been out visiting my Mama in McDougald. When we got back to Oxford Manor, my children went straight over to the next-door parking lot, where they knew that their friends would be out playing. I went into the house, not thinking of anything much. But no sooner had I gone into the kitchen than I heard a neighbor yelling from outside. "Emma! You have to come out. Your house is on fire!"

This time, the culprit turned out to be faulty electrical wiring. Emma's unit and the two adjoining ones were destroyed.

Emma asked the Housing Authority to send her back to McDougald Terrace if at all possible. Soon, she learned that her wish had been granted. She would be able to go back to her old friends, and of course her mother. Emma was particularly anxious to be near her mother, because Anna's health had gone into a steep decline. She had never been well since the shooting incident in 1963, but recently she had been diagnosed with diabetes, and her body had become prey to infections. In a terrible blow to her prospects for recovery, an infection led to gangrene and forced the amputation of both of her legs. Anna was confined to a wheelchair for the rest of her life.

Emma was given an apartment in the same block she had lived in before. This time she was right across from her mother's unit. In spite of her anxiety about her mother's health, Emma was at least happy to be living close to her again. And she was glad, too, to be back with her old friends and drinking partners.

Robert was happy, too — until Emma's children reported to her that they had seen him hiding something on a high shelf in her bedroom.

I went and took the kitchen chair upstairs and looked in the back of that closet. I saw something rolled up — needles and little glass things. So what the kids had told me was true! I went straight back down and called 911. I told them that I had a boyfriend who was keeping drug paraphernalia in my house, and would they please come and get him. The police came and I told them where to look. They got the stuff down. I said it belonged to him. Even Anna said so. I had no needle marks in me, so they said to Robert, "Well, Sir, we really can't say it's yours, but she wants you out of the house." So they waited while he got his stuff. Robert had never thought I would really make good on my threat. As he left the house, he said, "Emma, you should be ashamed." But to this day, he's still doing drugs.

Chapter 4

Legacies

By 1980, Emma had been living in the Durham housing projects for a decade. Her children had grown up in the projects.

They had been built with high hopes. They were intended to provide a much higher standard of housing for poor citizens of Durham than the dilapidated homes that many of them came from. But the effects were very far from the original ideas of the optimistic planners, and far also from the hopes of the displaced black families. Throughout the United States, public housing projects became a byword for poverty, deprivation, violence, drug abuse, and crime. Compared to the grim high-rises of some inner-city projects, Durham's public housing projects were green, spacious, and relatively comfortable. The city's public housing facilities were adequately maintained in spite of the challenges of tight budgets, mediocre management, and rapid depreciation. Compared with many, the Durham public housing projects could be deemed a success. But the Durham projects also fit the nationwide pattern in many ways.

By concentrating the city's poor into a few well-defined neighborhoods, the projects perpetuated the city's legacies of segregation and separation. Because of their poverty, the residents of the projects had little claim on city resources such as parks and recreational facilities, schools, and infrastructural investment. Because of their poverty they were unable to attract businesses, banks, retailers, or grocery stores. They had to travel further, pay more, and face the humiliation of being rejected for loan applications, credit cards, and mortgages.

By concentrating the poor, the projects also concentrated the problems of poverty — broken families, neglected children, drugs, violence, and school dropout. And by concentrating the poor, the projects increased the stigma of poverty. They led the residents to accept as a matter of course that their communities should be branded by a frightened public as hotbeds of crime, that their residents should be subject to frequent stops and searches by the police, and that they should be allowed to become a haven for drug dealers and gang organizers.

Emma's neighborhood fit the pattern of poverty and stigma painfully well. A 1975 study showed that it had the lowest median family income — under $6,000 per year — in the city of Durham. It also had one of the lowest educational levels — less than 45 percent of adults had completed high school. It had one of the lowest levels of park and recreational facilities, and it was one of the neighborhoods with the greatest number of arrests for crimes such as larceny and forcible entry.[1]

Ironically, because of the concentration of poor families in the projects and inner-city neighborhoods, and the white flight to the suburbs that took place throughout the 1970s and 1980s, Durham remained almost as segregated as it had been during the peak years of Jim Crow. In 1965 there had been 14,700 students in the city's newly desegregated school system — 55 percent of them white. Throughout the 1970s and 1980s, the city worked to integrate its schools, but even as the city's population grew, the overall number of students in its school system declined, as white families fled to the suburbs or placed their children in private schools. By the 1980s, no matter what the city did to integrate the schools, there were not enough white children left in the system to make desegregation meaningful. In 1992, when the Durham city school system merged with the county system, 91 percent of the city's eight thousand remaining public school students were black.[2] Many of the schools were failing across a broad range of standardized measures. For Emma's children, the reality of growing up in the 1970s and 1980s was a society as thoroughly segregated and discriminatory as it had been during the Jim Crow era.

Emma had grown up in a separate universe from white people, but she had been surrounded by a vibrant black community that offered her a sense of security and belonging. Her world had been shot through with violence and abuse, but it was still a world in which families supported their children with love and labor. The sense of community did not disappear with the move to the projects. Quite the reverse, the concentration of poor black families in a demarcated geographic space led to a new sense of togetherness and shared experience. Emma's friendships in the projects were the deepest and most meaningful of her life. Emma also became involved in community organizing: her commitment to this close-knit community led her to stand for election as secretary of the Tenants' Steering Committee.

Emma was on the steering committee for three years. In some ways, her involvement with this important community organization was empowering. Even before her election, Emma hadn't hesitated to speak out if she saw money being squandered, or tenants deprived of basic amenities. Indeed, it was her energy in revitalizing the neighborhood's landscape management that got her elected in the first place. Once she was on the committee she was able to fight for improved amenities, such as new cabinets and stoves for the units' kitchens. Her most important achievement was the establishment of a drug addiction clinic at the neighborhood recreation center. This was Emma's project from the beginning. Emma formed a subcommittee, and she and her friends passed out flyers persuading their neighbors to get behind the project and give it their support. They submitted an application for a grant from the city, which they received. Eventually they were successful in opening the new clinic, staffed by volunteer professionals who offered counseling services on overcoming addiction.

But the experience was also very disillusioning. Emma had not been on the committee long before she realized that much of the money being received from the city and the federal Department of Housing and Urban Development was being misspent, or even stolen. She became aware that members of her committee were falsifying records in order to cover up the disappearance of funds, and failing to provide important services for which they had received money. Meanwhile, the committee would treat itself to excursions and parties at the expense of the tenants who were in need of its services. Emma wanted to speak out about the abuses, but she was afraid that she would herself be implicated if there was an investigation, so she kept quiet.

And the society of the projects — together with many of the other poor neighborhoods of East Durham — was increasingly coming under pressure from the new scourges of the 1980s and 1990s: drugs, gangs, and illegal guns. In the mid–1980s, crack cocaine quickly spread as the drug of choice for poor, unemployed men and women in search of a quick high. Cheap, widely available, and easily ingested, crack produced an intense, instant high that gave its users a sense of euphoria and happiness that was not offered by any other aspect of their lives. The downside was that the high lasted only a short time, leading to a pressing urge to repeat the experience. Addiction became the new scourge of the urban poor. Vulnerable women who fell prey to drug addiction were liable to feed their habit at the expense of their own children.

In the 1990s, gangs grew in size and influence as they sought to control the lucrative trade. Guns became the new mark of status and self-respect. The number of shootings in Durham began to climb, until by the mid–1990s, three or four people — mostly young black men — were being shot every week. The murder rate, which had averaged around sixteen per year in the 1980s, almost doubled to an average of twenty-nine per year in the mid–1990s. The gangs offered structure, a sense of belonging, and even love to children who had never experienced those things at home. But they exacted a terrible toll in their debased currencies of drugs, violence and death.

As the projects became a byword for drug pushers and gang violence, the city's growing middle classes did their best to tune out their very existence. The poor black neighborhoods were geographically separate. There was no reason for white middle-class citizens to go near them. As Durham's murder rate climbed during the 1990s, the professionals in charge of crafting the city's progressive image reassured new residents and would-be investors that the crime problems were restricted to a few neighborhoods, that it was mostly poor black people killing other poor black people — nothing for of the comfortable middle classes to worry about. And so the middle-class community turned its back on the problems of its neighbors. Sometimes in comfortable white neighborhoods like Trinity Park and Forest Hills the residents would hear gunshots echoing out of East Durham. They would stir uneasily in their beds. But then they would remember that the violence belonged to a world apart from their own. They would check on their children sleeping safely and comfortably in their well-appointed rooms, and they would try and forget what they had heard. Meanwhile, in the black and Latino neighborhoods just a mile to the east, a man's life was worth no more than three lines of print on one of the back pages of the local newspaper.

Emma's children grew up in the projects, their lives touched by a variety of legacies, many of them toxic. In the womb, several of them suffered from their mother's addiction to alcohol and tobacco. As infants, they saw their mother beaten and abused. Their fathers disappeared early in their lives. The men who took their place carried guns and knives. As the children grew older, they were forced into the city's lowest-performing schools. They were socialized into a culture of rough justice and frequent brutality. They learned to distrust the police and anyone in authority. They were exposed to a world of drugs and crime. And they lived with the expectation of discrimination and failure stamped on their brows like the mark of Cain.

There were other legacies, too, that were more benign. In spite of her difficult circumstances, Emma never let any of her children go hungry. All of them knew the warmth of a mother's love. They were surrounded by a community that, while sometimes harsh and violent, could also be loving and caring. They had ready access to warm friendships. What they lacked was opportunity — the opportunity to set sail on the rising tide of Durham's growing prosperity.

In 1981, Emma enrolled in classes at Durham Tech to study for her GED. She had wanted to complete her education ever since being expelled from school at the age of thirteen. Ten years earlier her friend Katherine had encouraged her to think that she could study for her GED — only to use her child-care services as an excuse to take Emma's son Jake away from her. Now Emma's mother told her about a free program at Durham Tech and encouraged her to enroll. Leaving her mother to take care of the children, Emma started going to classes again four evenings a week. She turned out to be an excellent student.

> *Even though I left school so young, I had never stopped reading. Of course a lot of it was comic books, but you'd be surprised how much you can learn from those. I improved my vocabulary through reading, and I learned a lot about the world too. Then as my brothers went through school I helped them with their homework. So even though I wasn't at school, I was still studying history and geography and things.*

Emma had a natural aptitude for the written word, and she passed the English test before she even started class. She also tested out of science. The remaining classes were in geography, history, and math. Of these, the only one she found at all hard was the math. But at the end of a month, she was able to pass all three subjects, completing her requirements for the GED. She even went on to take a few college-level of classes in pharmacology, but increasingly overwhelming difficulties in her life soon forced her to give those up.

Outside the classroom, Emma's life was rapidly veering out of control. She had five children at home ranging in age from five to twelve; and she was pregnant again. Life at home was chaotic and bitter. Her relationship with Robert, the father of two of her children, had deteriorated into a nightmare of mutual distrust. Emma was engaged in a battle with Robert over his drug habits and his infidelity. Schooled by one abusive relationship after another, Emma in turn became an abuser, scolding and belittling her weak and cowardly boyfriend. Emma's children were growing up in a family at war, and it was a matter of time before the wounds began to open.

The father of Emma's unborn child was not Robert, but Don, a man with whom Emma had begun having an affair out of despair at the wreck of her relationship with her partner. Don was the son of a beautician, a lady who styled the hair of many of the women in the neighborhood out of her home in McDougald, right next door to Emma. Both Emma and her mother were customers, so Emma had known Don for years. He was a gentle man, never married. He wanted Emma to leave Robert and marry him.

He was frustrated because I wouldn't commit to him. He kept on coming round. But something told me it wasn't a good idea. Something was warning me. His Mama and I were real good friends. I knew a lot about him through her. He was into stuff that I wasn't into. He had some habits. I'd wised up enough to look and realize. Most of my life I've been taking care of someone. I didn't even know what reefer looked like, and I'd never heard of crack. Even if someone I knew was on stuff, I probably wouldn't have noticed unless someone told me or I actually caught them taking it. But with Don I had eyes to see. And I definitely didn't want to be involved with anyone who was taking drugs. I had no time, I had five kids, I had no time to nurse no drug addicts. I'd rather be hurt a bit one way than a whole lot the other.

Still, Emma had a child with Don: Michael, born in 1981. He was born at one of the lowest periods in Emma's life. She felt little love for his father, and even less for the man that she lived with — a man who preferred to live with the fiction that the child was his rather than face the reality of betrayal and the collapse of his relationship with Emma. Michael was Emma's ninth child, and her body was already starting to suffer the consequences of a lifetime of pregnancy, alcoholism and abuse. Shortly after his birth, Emma was diagnosed with ovarian cysts, and she underwent a hysterectomy. Michael was to be her last child. But in spite of all the problems surrounding his birth, he was also her most loved — until he died in an apartment parking lot with five bullets to his head and chest.

All through her twenties, Emma had been drinking heavily. She drank and smoked through one pregnancy after another, unaware of what effects her addictions might be having on her children. By the beginning of the 1980s, Emma had learned enough to stop drinking through her last pregnancy. But once Michael was born she took up the habit again. The drink helped her get through her days of rage and despair, but it forced her to give up her dreams of higher education.

> *I started drinking again after Michael was born, and it was downhill from there. Every time I started a new class I would drink myself out of it. I was getting a Pell Grant to attend the classes, and I know I was capable of doing the work. But the drink put me right out of it. I would start a class and never finish it. Perhaps the drinking was an excuse to quit; I don't know. I didn't believe in myself as much as I should have.*

Emma's drinking and her chaotic family life were also exacting an emotional toll on her children. One after another, they began showing symptoms of emotional and psychological distress — problems that have dogged them for their entire lives. Of the six children that Emma raised, not one escaped the problems of their troubled environment.

The trouble started with Brianna.

The first few years of Brianna's life seemed happy enough. She was well adjusted as a small child, and she did well in her early years at school. In fact, she was a charming and mischievous little girl who was much loved in the neighborhood. She was known most of all for her amazing gift of the gab. The words flowed from her in a constant stream, funny and cheeky and outrageous. She was a champion storyteller — she could spin the wildest yarn and make her listeners believe her. She seemed to get a deep pleasure from the tales that she wove, and she became so caught up in them that she herself came to believe them. Her stories involved everyone that she knew. No secret was safe with her. "Brianna can't hold water," people would say.

> *She told on everyone. Her job was to tell everything she saw or heard. She'd tell me, she'd tell her brother. Or she'd tell others — I wish she'd confined herself! Sometimes she talked so fast she'd tell on herself. If you want someone to know something you can tell her and they'll get the message! And you had to be careful when dealing with her. She'd start out telling the truth but by the time she actually got through, it would be like another fairy tale.*

Lots of children told stories. But Brianna's special gift was to blur the boundaries between fantasy and reality. She spun a web of consequences with her constant storytelling — a web that eventually was to catch Emma and Brianna herself in its viscous threads.

Brianna dreamed of a world in which she would be the center of attention, in which she would be cosseted with gifts of new clothes and toys. She imagined herself in a family where she was the special one, and where her mother was not constantly battling to make a few dollars stretch to the needs of six children. And when she talked to her friends at school, she thought she saw the possibility of this new world open up. One of the children in her class had told her that if a child was taken into foster care, she would be showered with presents and new clothes. The naive ten-year-old decided that she would make a bid for such a life.

"Mama," she said one day, "I'm going to tell my teachers you've been beating me so that they'll send me into foster care."

"Girl, if you don't get outta here, I'll show you what a beating is!"

Brianna's comments hurt Emma, because she had been making sacrifices to provide for her children, and they lacked for nothing essential. But she never expected that Brianna would make good on her threat. A few days later, Emma had a visit from the Social Services department.

I don't know what Brianna told them about me. I wouldn't have been surprised no matter what she accused me of. By the time they talked to me they'd already made up their minds. I went into it in defender mode.

Emma had five other children to worry about, including a newborn. It was as much as she could do to hold on to the bare necessities of life. And she was worried that the Social Services department might try and take her other children. In the end, she agreed to give up Brianna, so long as she would be allowed to keep all the others.

Brianna found that foster care was not at all what she had bargained for. Her foster parents were kind people. They took Brianna in at the beginning of the summer, and shortly afterward they took her on a summer vacation — something that Emma had never in her life been able to afford — thinking that it would be a way to form a bond with their new charge. But as soon as they arrived at their destination, Brianna ran away. Emma got a phone call at midnight saying that she had gone missing. Emma had no car, and she did not know where the family was. So there was nothing she could do but stay on the other end of the telephone and hope for good news.

Brianna was found later that night. She had walked on her own to the bus station and had tried to board a bus back to Durham. Seeing a ten-year-old girl wandering alone at night, the dispatcher had called the police, who eventually brought Brianna back to her foster family.

I didn't have money to take my children on big trips. But I would take them to places that didn't cost money — we'd go to the Regal Theater, and to the cafes, and to the place where I got my hair fixed. They loved music, and in one of those cafes someone had fixed the jukebox so you didn't have to put money in. We had those kinds of things together. That's what she missed when they put her in a home.

In the end, Brianna stayed in the foster care system for only a year. During that year she changed homes several times as one foster family after another found her more than they could manage. At first she was allowed frequent visits with Emma, but after the visits she would always behave recklessly and destructively, and eventually her foster parents asked that the visits be suspended. Then she began running away, showing up on Emma's doorstep whenever she was able to escape. But the system didn't allow her just to change her mind about going into care.

> *The rules were that if she ran away to my house, I had to dial 911 and contact the social worker on call. So that's what I did. They came to get her in a police car. She resisted, so they put her in leg restraints. It was heartrending watching her being dragged away, kicking and screaming. She was really paying for her rash words.*

Eventually, Emma petitioned the Social Services department to return her daughter to her. It was obvious that she was not doing well in foster care, and the department, which had been monitoring Emma, was by this time convinced that she was not mistreating her kids. So after a year, Brianna came home.

But Brianna's troubles were far from over. After her return to Emma's house, her behavior was wilder than ever. She went to school only sporadically, and by the eighth grade she dropped out altogether. She began coming home from her friends' houses with red eyes.

> *I knew something was wrong. I thought it was alcohol. I'd never seen or smelled marijuana before. So when she came in with those red eyes I thought she'd been crying. Then I'd put her clothes in the washing machine. I'd tell her, "I don't know what you've been doing, but your clothes smell bad. In the end some of my friends told me that was the marijuana smell.*

Then, in 1985, Brianna got pregnant. She was thirteen years old.

She was a frequent visitor at the house of Gemma, a neighbor and an old and close friend of Emma's. Gemma had a daughter who was close to Brianna's age. Emma trusted her friend to take care of Brianna, but unbeknownst to Emma, Gemma was cruelly betraying her. Gemma had another pair of frequent visitors, two brothers called Jack and Jim. The brothers were distantly related to her, and she welcomed them as drinking partners, even though Jack was severely retarded. Gemma, out of drunkenness and malice, encouraged Jack to have sex with thirteen-year-old Brianna. Jack didn't know any better. Brianna, curious and excited, went along with it. Gemma encouraged her by plying her with drink. Before too long her sleepovers with Gemma had turned into nights of debauchery.

Brianna barely understood what was happening to her. She was a clever child, but still naive about the realities of adult life. It was only when Emma noticed Brianna's missed periods that the truth finally began to come out.

> I blame myself for not seeing what was going on. I let Brianna know that it wasn't really her fault. I trained her to respect grown people. I didn't give her the weapons to defend herself against something like this. I didn't think she would need them. It's Gemma who's at fault. That's who I blame the most. I trusted my friend. It was a terrible betrayal—the one thing I wasn't even looking for. I even went and cried on her shoulder when I found out—little knowing that she herself was the perpetrator!

Emma turned her friend in to the authorities, and Jack was sent to prison for several months. But Gemma walked away without any penalty.

In 1985, at the age of thirty-six, Emma became a grandmother. Now her problems and responsibilities extended beyond her own children to the next generation. Her first grandchild was a boy, named Tyrone. Just a year later Brianna conceived her second child, Ebony, and by the time Brianna was nineteen she had four children, each by a different father. She never attended school past the eighth grade. From the age of fifteen, she was addicted to crack cocaine.

Brianna's problems were the first squall in a storm of parenting nightmares that continued throughout the 1980s and that still haunt Emma's life to this day.

Tamara was next.

Tamara, who entered middle school in 1981, had been a fighter from an early age.

> Out of all my children she was the most mischievous—she got into trouble the most. She would fight at the drop of a hat. I had to keep her on punishment a lot. But she had a lot of friends. She played hard.

Tamara had little interest in school, and she became adept at playing truant.

I had to go to the school a lot. It was either fighting or forged notes. The teacher realized that the notes [that Tamara gave to excuse herself from attendance] *were not in my handwriting. And they'd ask me, and I'd say, "I haven't seen no note." I would take her to school myself, but I don't know how, she somehow got out of the building. She'd be at my mom's house while I was busy doing my chores. She was a good student—she could get As and Bs when she showed up for class. But she just didn't want to be there. Her friends from the neighborhood were probably missing school too.*

By the eighth grade, Tamara had quit going to school altogether. The school authorities finally sent the truant officers to Emma's house. Emma was cooking a meal when the officers pounded on the door. When she opened it, they showed her a warrant for her own arrest. Truancy was (and is) an offense in Durham: a parent who fails to make a good-faith effort to comply with North Carolina's Compulsory Attendance Law can be charged with a Class 1 misdemeanor — the most severe category below a felony. Depending on the parent's previous record, this could potentially result in a sentence of up to several months in jail.

In spite of the many troubles in her life, Emma had never to that point had to endure the humiliation of being arrested in her own home.

I was so scared. The neighbors said don't worry — but the police, they put handcuffs on me! That's got to be the most humiliating thing I could think of, getting into the back of that car in front of my neighbors. My children were just standing there crying. The police had never even been to our house, and now they were arresting me in front of my children and taking me to jail!

Emma asked her neighbors to watch out for her children until she could get out on bond. Her mother, alerted at home, quickly arranged for a bondsman to meet Emma at the jail, and in the end she was only incarcerated for the length of time it took to do her paperwork and be photographed. And when she eventually had her court appearance,

That judge just told them off. He congratulated them on taking a parent that's really doing her best, taking her daughter by the hand to school every morning. It's not her Mama's fault if the child runs off after that. Why don't they go after some of the parents who really

don't do anything? I didn't want to be arrested, but I feel like justice prevailed. I knew how hard I'd worked. When the judge said those things, I was so glad, I didn't know what in the world to do.

After the arrest, the authorities stopped bothering Emma about Tamara, but Emma's daughter never went back to school. She was still too young to go out to work, so Emma let her stay home, making her help with the chores. Most of Tamara's friends had also dropped out of school, so she had no shortage of playmates.

She wasn't after the boys. In fact she was still sort of a tomboy herself. Usually if she was with a boy it was in a fight. I had some very sharp knives, steak knives. One day I couldn't find one of them. She was carrying it around in her back pocket! I don't know if it's hereditary or what, but I would guess she got it from her daddy [Anthony]. She looks just like he did. They could walk down the street and everyone would know she was his daughter. She was another him in girl form. She would do the same things as he did, too.

Tamara was fiercely protective of her siblings, particularly her brother Laurence, who found it much harder than she did to take care of himself.

Laurence was an introvert. He didn't have a gang of friends. He never wanted to hang around. He got picked on through middle school. I often had to go to the school to talk to teachers and parents of the boys who were bullying him.

Increasingly, Laurence began avoiding school altogether. Whenever he could get away with it he would stay home and hang out with Tamara and her friends — or he would just stay in his room and brood. Unlike Tamara, who would take out her frustrations in violent action, Laurence had no outlets for his feelings. Emma was so consumed by the welter of problems in her life that she could not see how disturbed he was becoming. Then one day he forced Emma to recognize it. Desperate feelings call for desperate acts.

I was downstairs calling him to come on down when I heard a big BOOM! My friend Nookie was there. It scared us so bad, we both ran up there. And there he was lying on the floor, half in and half out of my closet. At first we thought it must be seizures. But then I saw the empty bottle of pills on the floor. He had taken all of my prescription tranquilizers. He had hidden himself in my closet and tried to kill himself. He had fallen over and broken the closet door. The pressure was more than I understood it to be. My other kids were so self-reliant. I come from the class where if someone hits you, you hit him back. But he needed something else—a safe haven, someone to understand. I didn't know the pressure was as tough as it was.

As if her problems with her three oldest children weren't enough, Emma now found herself raising her own grandchildren, the oldest of whom was only four years younger than her youngest son. Tyrone was a challenge from the beginning. From his infancy it was apparent that—like his father—he suffered from cognitive impairment. He failed to develop like other children his age, and as a result he needed constant care—care that his own mother was not available to give him. Brianna, in fact, was barely at home. After leaving school, she enrolled in the Job Corps as an alternative to high school. The program sent her away on work assignments, but she was never committed to seeing them through. When she returned home, she was with her friends, many of whom encouraged her to drink and experiment with drugs. While she was still in her teens, Emma became convinced that Brianna had a serious substance abuse problem, and several times Emma enrolled her daughter in rehabilitation programs. Meanwhile, the care of her grandchildren fell to her.

In her later teens, Brianna took up with a young man Emma could not stand. Emma was convinced he was a drug dealer, and he in turn disliked Emma. Brianna had a child by him, Tyreese, her fourth, and from that moment Tyreese's father seemed to be intent on getting rid of all her other children from her life.

One day, a call came from Social Services. There had been a complaint about drug activity in Emma's house. Someone had informed them that Emma, who was acting as the main caregiver for the children, was a drug addict and not fit to raise children. Emma suspects Brianna's boyfriend. Although they had no evidence against her, the department took the allegations seriously. The officers were well aware of the issues in her household. In the end, they persuaded Brianna to sign three of her children away, and they were put into care. The fourth, Tyreese, was raised by his aunt.

Tyrone went to a special home for children with disabilities. The two middle children, Ebony and Lavaughan, were placed together into the home of an elderly foster parent, Mrs. James. Eventually, she adopted them both and raised them to adulthood.

Like Brianna, Laurence dropped out of middle school and went into the Job Corps, a federal residential program for at-risk teens and young adults that aims to provide core vocational skills through a mixture of academic and hands-on experience. Laurence started the program in the North Carolina mountains and then moved to Gwendolyn. Unlike his sister, he loved the program and did well in it. By the time he came back to Durham, he had gained enormously in confidence and practical skills. The Corps helped him secure a job in Durham.

> He was working in one of the kitchens at Duke. They loved him there! He'd bring me treats. He knew I loved shaved ham, so he was always finding a way to carry some home, and he'd bring it to me.

It seemed as though Laurence's life was on a more even keel. But one day he was invited to a party where someone gave him some crack cocaine to smoke. Emma believes that it only took that one experience to work an irreversible transformation on her son.

> He was in and out of treatment after that. It messed him up mentally. He worked for years — it looked like he was doing good. But then suddenly he'd go on a spree again. When he worked, he worked well. But now he'd do anything for a job.

And it wasn't long before Tamara, too, began to get involved in drugs.

> Her and Laurence got together with some people that had just come to the area. They'd come home and their eyes were just so red. I didn't smell alcohol. She and her brother had started to experiment with reefer.

Once Emma realized what her daughter was up to, she did her best to stop her. But as Tamara got older she began spending more and more time away from home. At first Emma worried about her absence, and once or twice she even called the police. But gradually she came to understand that she had lost her hold on her daughter. Tamara knew that Emma would recognize the signs if she was on drugs, so she stayed away until she was clean again. When she was at home, she was well behaved — she helped her mother clean the house and behaved like a model daughter. But if Emma called her while Tamara was away, Emma would recognize the strange sound to her voice. She realized that her daughter was staying away because she was high, to avoid upsetting her mother.

Those drugs, they will change your perception on the inside and your appearance on the outside.

Laurence in particular changed noticeably when he was on drugs. His mouth would shift subtly to one side, and it would acquire an uncontrollable tic.

Like her brother and sister, Tamara began experimenting with all sorts of drugs, including crack. Once, Emma got a phone call saying that her daughter was in a hysterical state.

She took some pills, and those pills had an effect on her. She began to see things crawling up the wall, and she was screaming and crying at her friend's house. They brought her home to me, and I was afraid of my own child. She was punching anyone that got close to her! And she was talking about aliens and stuff. All I knew to do was to call an ambulance. They asked me what she'd taken, but I had no idea. Later I learned it was a pill called "black beauty" in combination with some other drug.

There was a wide range of drugs available to the children. Tamara had lots of friends, many of them men who were happy to give her a cheap hit. A "ten-cent" piece of crack cocaine sold for only ten dollars, a "rock" for twenty dollars.

People just liked Tamara. They'd come and tell her, "Hey, I've got something." You'd see their hand balled up tight; that's what they were holding. It would make me so mad. It was a catalyst; she just had to go with it. She had no problem getting what she wanted.

Indeed, the drug culture permeated their neighborhood. Increasingly, Emma's own friends were also getting high on drugs.

> There was a girl I had known since childhood in Hayti. We called her Lulu. She got into those drugs, and her mouth turned permanently to the side. It never came back.

Emma felt that her children were following a dangerous path.

> I didn't know much about drugs, but I knew that they were taking a big risk. I wondered what they were thinking of, after all I'd tried to teach them, after all the punishment. After all that, they were silly enough to get into those drugs. I don't think any of my children have ever done the needle, but apart from that, I think cocaine is the most powerful drug there is. It takes a lot to get off of it. My belief is that cocaine is not only a worldly drug, but it also has supernatural tendencies. I believe in Satan; I know he is real in my mind. You could take cocaine just one time and get the habit.

Eventually the drugs put both Laurence and Tamara into the mental hospital. The North Carolina state mental facility at Butner—a grim fortress right next door to the state prison, and with much of the same feel—had a drug rehabilitation facility, and after Tamara had a particularly bad spell, Emma went to the county Social Services administration and filled out the paperwork to have her daughter committed.

> She was incorrigible. It wasn't a particular incident. It was a culmination of things, where it looked like no matter which way you bent, it wasn't going to be enough. This seemed like the only way to get her some help.

It wasn't only the growing evidence of a serious drug problem. Emma was also deeply concerned about her daughter's violent tendencies. Still a teenager, Tamara always carried a switchblade with her, and if she felt provoked she would not hesitate to draw it, even against men who were much bigger than her. Emma was really worried that Tamara might hurt someone seriously, or get hurt herself.

Tamara's period of treatment had limited results.

> It worked for about six months after she got out. But it didn't last. It's real hard to resist cocaine. It's powerful on its own. It doesn't need

anything to help it. Not when you're living in a neighborhood where the dealers are your friends. They would have cookouts, play loud music, and nobody would call the police. I think selling is worse than being an addict. Addicts can't help themselves. Dealers have no excuse. The people that sell that poison hurt the neighborhood; they brought us down, they made our children suffer. When you sell a Mama that rock and she gives you money she was supposed to pay the rent with, you might as well have been selling to the kids. They'll even take food stamps! Yes, even after they went to cards instead of stamps. Those people are smart. The father of one of my grandchildren, he was talking one day—he had eight food stamp cards in his pocket. He's not a drug dealer, but he'll buy those cards off the drug addicts—he'll give them $50 for a $100 card.

Emma has had to have Laurence hospitalized several times for his own safety—and hers. During bouts of hallucination, Laurence would hold on to Emma so hard that she was afraid she would be injured. Once, she called the police and had him arrested.

He stole my car. My keys were sitting there on the table, and he just took them. I called 911 on him. I needed some semblance of order with all those kids. I started being a parent at fourteen. I didn't have all the tools I needed. My own parent hadn't even finished parenting me! That leaves you with less to give them.

One day, Emma was babysitting no fewer than eight children and grandchildren, including Brianna's three children as well as Michael and several neighbor children. Suddenly Brianna rushed into the house, shouting to Emma, "Close all the doors and lock them." Brianna, wide eyed and terrified, told Emma that she was being followed.

"I don't know why he's chasing me," she cried. "Mama, I didn't do anything to him. You've got to help me."

Emma found herself wishing that she had never let her daughter into the house—and then she felt guilty for thinking that of her own daughter. But she was responsible for eight children. She could not afford to let her house become a battleground between Brianna and her enemies.

A few minutes later, there was a loud banging on the door. Brianna ran upstairs and locked herself in Emma's bedroom.

"If you don't open the door, I'm going to shoot right through it," said a male voice.

Terrified, Emma opened the door, and a young man thrust his way in, brandishing a gun. He was obviously high on drugs.

"Where is she?" he demanded.

Emma told him that her daughter had left out of the back door, but the intruder clearly didn't believe her.

> He told me he and my daughter had gotten high together and he also let her have some drugs that she was supposed to pay for, but she fooled him and he was going to get her. She told him she could get the money from her mother, and he really believed her. He said at first he thought she was a nice girl. I tried to sympathize with him and told him if I had the money I would pay him. I also appealed to his decent side: about the children and how we had not done anything to him and we were not responsible for what my daughter had done. But in his state, he could only think about how she had made a fool of him and how much he wanted to get her.

Finally, Emma told him that she had to go to the bathroom, and after slamming the bathroom door, she sneaked into her bedroom, where Brianna was cowering in a corner, and dialed 911.

When she heard the sirens approach her house, Emma looked the young intruder in the eye. Both of them understood that she had betrayed him.

> I was so afraid I could hardly breathe. I jumped up and started to the door. I just knew he was going to shoot me in the back. I heard movement behind me. I didn't stop. When I reached the door I opened it as quickly as possible. The police rushed in and immediately handcuffed him.
>
> When there is an addict in the family, it not only affects the person, but everyone connected with them.

As if these problems weren't enough to deal with, Emma's most troubled child of all was her youngest daughter, Anna.

Like her older siblings, there was little in Anna's early childhood to hint at the troubles to come.

She was a homebody. She liked to play out in the yard or in the house. She didn't take to a lot of people. Not just anyone could pick her up as a toddler. But she was a sweet child, a mama's child. She was always staying very close to me.

But like her older sister, Anna took up with the wrong boys and found herself pregnant while she was still in her early teens. Like Brianna, Anna met the father of her child while she was playing at a friend's house. Once again, Emma was let down by a neighbor mother who should have known better.

His name was Junior, and he was nineteen years old. He lived a few blocks away, outside the housing project, with his father and sister, but he was a frequent visitor at Anna's friend's house, where there was a constant stream of visitors — no doubt that's what made the house so appealing to young Anna. That, and the lack of supervision.

Once again, Emma had to make the discovery that her daughter was missing her periods.

Lord, I was so upset! I let Junior and his dad know it, too! I just— it took me a while to get over it. Even thinking about it right now. That was the turning point for her.

Emma had raised her children not to consider abortion as an option. Perhaps because of her Catholic family background, Emma herself had been brought up opposed to the idea. So Anna had to live with the consequences. She was very sick during her pregnancy, and she dropped out of school, never to return. Her daughter Tekeysia was born in 1989. Anna was fifteen years old.

Shortly after Tekeysia's birth, Anna met Sammy.

I found out later that he'd not been long out of prison, but when I first met him my only objection was that he seemed a little old for her. He was more experienced—he tried to hide it, but it came out sometimes when I talked to him. I wondered at the time.

Sammy quickly became Anna's lover. Emma suspects that her neighbor allowed the two to meet and make love in her house — she usually had a good idea where her daughter was, and she was pretty sure that she was not going to meet Sammy in a motel. Before long Anna was pregnant again. Her second child, Bethany, was born barely a year after Tekeysia.

After Bethany's birth, Anna applied to the city authorities for her own apartment, and eventually she was given one in the Few Gardens project.

> *Lord, I don't know what happened over there because she changed completely. As sweet as she had always been, I never thought she'd turn into something like that. She just went wild when she got her freedom. I'd go to her house and it was full of people. I'd call, and strangers would answer. Her kids would call me and cry, "We're hungry!" I'll always wonder if something happened to her in Few Gardens. Everything changed. I didn't know what to think. I've never seen anyone change like that.*

Anna was to go on to bear a total of seven children, all by different fathers. The effort to save them from their own toxic inheritance has been among the defining struggles of Emma's middle age, and its consequences continue to haunt her today.

Meanwhile, Emma's relationship with her partner Robert finally ended. For years, the couple had hardly spoken except to fight. When the end finally came, it wasn't over drugs but a woman.

> *One day Robert comes and tells me that he has this friend. Her name was Ashley, and she didn't have no place to stay. He wanted to let her sleep at my place. Well, I took him at his word, and this Ashley comes and sleeps on the couch in my living room. Only it didn't take long for me to realize that he was offering her a whole lot more than a couch to sleep on. Robert started hanging out with her down there, and every time I came into the room, I'd see him innocently reading the paper. Well I knew there was something very wrong. Robert didn't read no paper! I'd never seen him read one before. He was trying to make a fool of me again.*

Once Emma realized what was going on, she told Ashley to leave. Ashley tried to brazen it out with Emma.

> *She said, "I'm going to tell Robert what you did to me!" And I replied, "That's okay. This apartment doesn't belong to Robert. It belongs to Emma."*

Even after Ashley left, Emma was not rid of her. Robert seemed to have come under her spell. A week or two later, Emma's friend Don told her that he had seen Robert and Ashley going together into a rooming house on Fayetteville Street.

> *Don drove me over, and what do I see but that Ashley, sitting in the window where everyone could see her. Well, I knew Robert had been visiting her there, and I was ready to have it out with her. I went storming up the stairs, ready to fight. But she heard me coming and ran into a neighbor's room.*

Now that Emma knew where Ashley and Robert were having their liaisons, she began visiting the house regularly, determined to catch Ashley and punish her. And eventually her patience was rewarded. One day she caught Ashley stepping out into the street, and she attacked her rival both verbally and physically.

> *Years later, Ashley apologized to me. She knew that what she was doing was wrong. But you know, although I was mad at her, I didn't really feel very jealous. I think by this time my feelings had changed so much for Robert. I knew in my heart that it was already over with him. We'd been together for so long that I just kept on doing the same thing. But I wasn't feeling the same. I wasn't attracted to him anymore, not in any intimate way. I really didn't care that much about him going with Ashley. What got me mad was the way he did things—bringing his girlfriend to my own house!*

When Emma finally threw Robert out, she began to understand how much he really cared about her. In spite of his affair with Ashley, he was devastated at the breakup with Emma. A little before their final breakup, he had come into some money: due to a pension scandal in the Housing Authority, some of the employees including Robert had received early lump-sum payments from the pension fund. Robert used the money to buy a car, and now that he was no longer living with Emma, he began sleeping in that car—and parking it right across the street from Emma's apartment. Nor was that his only strategy to haunt Emma. Never a very attentive father while living with his family, he now began paying regular visits to his children at their mother's house.

I told him, if you want to see them, then get yourself a room and take them there to visit. And I started limiting the time that he could spend with them in my house. I was convinced that all these visits were just a strategy to push himself back into my life. He never did any of the things a good father should do. He never paid any support for his own children.

After Emma's final breakup with Robert, she continued seeing Don for a while. But her relationship with him had never been very deep. His fatherhood of Emma's youngest child Michael was the tie that kept them closest together. But Don and Emma never lived together, and by the mid–1980s, Emma was ready to move on. It was at that time that she had an unexpected visit. The visitor was her first lover, David.

He was living in my community and I didn't even know it. I knew nothing about him in all of these years. But he said, "I keep up with you." Just like that. Well, it snowballed from there. I don't know if my feelings for him ever really went away. I left him really from necessity. I can't explain it, but we got together, and very quickly we were serious.

For the third time in her life, Emma traveled to South Carolina, the home of her forebears, to get married.

When she was only a child of thirteen, Emma had been mesmerized by David. He was her first love, and in spite of all the violence and betrayal, Emma thinks of him to this day as the true love of her life. Her feelings for him were not such as could be rationally explained. Years earlier, Emma's instinct for self-preservation had battled against her impulsive love of this man, and survival had won. She had left him and moved on with her life. Now, twenty-five years later, she allowed her heart to prevail. She tried desperately to believe that David was a changed man.

But it turned out that the one who had changed was Emma. David quickly resumed the old abusive pattern of their relationship. He cheated on Emma, and he beat her, expecting to see her cringe and cower. Emma loved David with all her heart, but she was never going to put up with this kind of mistreatment again.

David had bought me a pistol, and after all of that abuse, I'd just about made up my mind to use it— on him. He knew it. He looked into my eyes and saw it. I had made up my mind not to be abused.

As it turned out, Emma did not have a chance to test her resolve. The summer of 1989 was a terrible time for Emma. In June her beloved mother died after years of poor health. Emma was devastated at her loss.

Then, in August, after only one year of marriage, David was run over and killed.

David had been visiting his mother's house. He and Emma had been planning to move into a house of their own, and that morning they had been finalizing the arrangements. No one knows exactly what happened after that.

A friend of mine, her son was going to the liquor store on Fayetteville Street, and he saw what happened. It seems like David was hit first by a car and then by a truck. He had gone into the store for his Mama. Someone said he was pushed. I'll never know what really happened. All I know is the outcome. His Mama and I rushed to Duke Hospital's emergency room. Oh, how I grew to hate that little room that they take you to.

For a while, Emma's life descended into a slough of despond. With no one to turn to, she was responsible for six adolescent and young adult lives, as well as a growing brood of grandchildren.

To make matters even worse, Emma also had to take on the care of her brother Junebug, who had suffered an appalling accident. All her life Junebug had been Emma's supporter and protector. But in 1982 he was hit by a car while crossing Alston Avenue and suffered severe injuries that left him mentally and physically impaired. He had to learn to walk and talk all over again, and even after he made some progress, he was still largely unable to look after himself. He was incontinent and had to wear diapers for several years. Then, just when he was showing signs of recovery, he was run over a second time, undoing much of the progress. Junebug, whom men had literally killed to be close to, now had no one to care for him except his sister. When Anna died, Junebug came to live with Emma in her crowded apartment.

143

In the midst of all these challenges, Emma suddenly and completely gave up drinking.

It just happened one night. I'd been drinking all day long, I'd put the children to bed, and I was all set to go on drinking into the evening. But somehow it just didn't taste right. I flushed it down the commode, and I was feeling that something just wasn't right! That night I really got down on my knees. I was down there for a long, long time, praying. I said, "Jesus, won't you take the taste of alcohol from me. I don't like it and I don't like what it does to me. Father, I need help." I was talking to Him just like I'm talking to you now. When I got back up off my knees, I went to bed. And the next day I did not realize I had not drunk anything till almost afternoon. I hadn't even wanted to drink. I've had none of the urges that some people get. God was really good to me on that one.

Emma's faith had always been important to her, but the ease with which she gave up alcohol (and later cigarettes) convinced her that she had a protector who would take care of her no matter what.

I have always believed in God. He has always been there for me — always. In my life I have been through things that no other living person could help me with. But the Lord is supreme, He would support me in my time of trial, and He would punish me and others for the things they did. Even if you don't believe in the spiritual, it doesn't matter, because God gets you. If we do something, we are going to pay. I did not go to church regularly after I turned to alcohol, but in my mind, I always knew that Jesus was beside me. And even if I wasn't in church or being preached to, I could always meditate on Jesus, and the more I did, the more I would feel His holy presence. I call Jesus Father, I call Him my parent, and I know that He loves me. I know He won't intentionally do me any harm. I lean on Him for understanding to the point that I can live happily.

However, Emma's triumph over alcoholism did not stop her health from taking a dramatic turn for the worse. She began feeling dizzy, and her vision became blurred. When she went to the doctor, the tests showed a blood sugar level over five hundred. For a while, Emma had to be hospitalized until the doctors were able to stabilize her sugar levels. The diagnosis of diabetes turned out to be the first in a cascade of physical ailments that were to turn Emma into an invalid well before her time.

> *It's not that I'd been leading such an unhealthy life. Physically I was in good shape. I wasn't overweight in those days. I was a really small girl in fact. With so many children I was always on the go, and that's one way I kept slim. Another was having a husband that beat my butt—that kept me in shape. I was always having to run from him! And I didn't drive, so I often had to walk places.*

Whatever the causes, Emma's diabetes was followed by diagnoses of heart disease, asthma, and a host of lesser complaints. Forced to stay at home and with her eating patterns disrupted by the diabetes, Emma began to gain weight. Eventually she put on over a hundred pounds, further compounding her health problems.

In spite of the darkness in her life, there was still plenty of love and laughter. Emma was supported by her many close friendships, several of which dated back to her childhood in Hayti. Her family remained close in spite of all the dislocations, and indeed she remained friendly even with the men who had formerly abused her. Tamara and Laurence's father remained close to his children, and after his release from prison, Emma remained on cordial terms with him for their sake. He continued paying child support while in prison and after his release. Anthony had two children by another woman, and Tamara eventually became close friends with her half brother and sister, even going to live with them for a while before her father's death in 2004.

Emma also forged closer ties with her extended family, based in Bennettsville, South Carolina. Her brother Lionel first went down there when one of their cousins got married. He was overwhelmed by the huge family circle that he was introduced to. Eventually the family extended a welcoming arm to Emma.

> *I met people who were named after others I knew. And the people had similar lifestyles and actions. You know, you could tell we were related. It's amazing, really, the way they would talk and describe things. I knew people who had the same mannerisms.*

Among the people Emma met was her great aunt Thelma. Thelma, who worked at a Dairy Queen in Bennettsville until she was almost eighty years old, knew everyone in the extended family. Emma became close not only to Thelma, but also to her niece Maggie, known in the family as Tootsie, and to Tootsie's children whom Thelma had helped to raise. Another family contact was Wilbur, a pastor who lived in Charlotte and who knew even the farther-flung members of the family. Wilbur helped Emma make contact with cousins in Virginia, New York, and Pennsylvania.

In September 1992, Emma married for the fourth time, to Jimmy Cheek. She remains married to him today.

Jimmy is Emma's cousin — the son of her Aunt Mary. He had grown up with his mother's family in Bennettsville. Emma had met him occasionally on family visits but did not know him intimately. When he was older, Jimmy's family moved to New York. Jimmy had never married, but he had one son from a previous relationship.

When he came into Emma's life, she was immediately drawn by his gentleness and respect for her. He was completely unlike the other men in her life. The fact that they were cousins gave them an added intimacy that made her feel very warm to him. At the time that she met him, Jimmy was engaged in a fight with his former employer over disability. He was a skilled carpenter, and while he was on a job, he had been in an accident: a pile of planks had fallen on his head, crushing several vertebrae in his back. Then, shortly afterward, his work truck had been involved in a wreck, injuring him further. The company claimed that all of the injury had been caused by the wreck, which they said was Jimmy's fault. Emma and Jimmy worked together to fight for his rights, hiring a lawyer and eventually winning a small settlement from the company (though he was never able to secure workmen's compensation). The experience brought them still closer together.

One night in October 1995, Junebug came home drunk. He had been drinking with his friends, who had thought it amusing even though they knew that he was much too impaired to deal with the effects of alcohol. Junebug showed up on Emma's doorstep swearing and shouting, and Emma refused to let him in. Junebug reacted by going to the neighbors and calling the police to complain about his sister's treatment. This was clearly the act of a drunken and mentally challenged person, but there was nothing criminal about it. When the police came, though, they placed him under arrest and clamped his wrists in handcuffs.

Emma was horrified to see this turn of events. She explained to them that her brother was disabled, but the police insisted on booking him "to teach him a lesson." They refused to take along his medicine, which he needed for his occasional seizures. They told Emma they had doctors at police headquarters in case one was needed, and they promised they would not allow him to come to any harm. As they took Junebug away, Emma cautioned them not to turn him loose without letting her know. "He hasn't committed a crime," she told them, "and he has the mind of a child."

I will never forget that Saturday afternoon, as they pulled off with him in the back of the car. He looked back at me standing on the front porch, and I had the strangest feeling.

It was a stormy night, and after Junebug was taken away it began to rain heavily. Emma sat at home worrying about the events of the evening. She was still awake when, near one in the morning, there was a banging on her door. It was a friend who had just been driving past Alston Avenue. He said he had seen a terrible accident, and the victim was Junebug. Emma's first reaction was disbelief— surely the police wouldn't have let him loose. But it was true. He had been walking in the rain on Alston Avenue, and he had been hit by the car of Mr. Street, the owner of a local store. The first car had knocked him into another, and by the time the emergency services arrived he was already dead.

The police didn't even apologize. In my mind even today, they were wrong. He was handicapped; he couldn't think for himself. They shouldn't have just turned him loose like that. But when I went to complain, they just sent me from one person to another. I even talked to the police chief, but they all passed the buck. I just got so tired of it.

At the same time, Emma was becoming increasingly worried about her daughter Anna. Anna was in her early twenties, and she was already far along the road to alcoholism. She had four children by this time, and all of them were suffering from abuse and neglect. Emma was becoming increasingly concerned that, like their cousins, they would be taken away from their mother and placed in the city's foster care system.

In the midst of all these problems, Jimmy — who had his own construction business — was offered a contract to work in Wilson, North Carolina, about seventy miles from Durham. Emma was willing to make the move. She had a cousin in Wilson — Anne, the daughter of her uncle Evander. Anne was a single woman with no brothers or sisters and only one daughter, and she pressed Emma to join her. Emma's bitterness after the death of Junebug helped her decide. Her only concern was that she would be further from her grandchildren and might be less able to protect them.

The move to Wilson went well. Michael quickly settled into his new school there, Fike High.

> *Michael was a real homebody in those days. He was home so much, you almost had to push him out. His cousin Alice, she was always trying to get him to know everyone she knew. She tried to get him connected, but it was hard, because Michael wasn't a walker. His feet gave him trouble. All the young people walked or rode bicycles, but Michael couldn't, or wouldn't. One day, Alice talked him into going with her to show him around. He had no idea he was supposed to walk! He came home early, took off his shoes, and soaked his feet. They hadn't even been able to get him to walk as far as the Piggly Wiggly! "Oh, man, my feet was hurting," he said. We laughed so much! We used to say that a butterfly couldn't land on his feet without it hurting.*

Soon after they moved, Tamara and Laurence joined them. They had been squatting in Emma's old apartment in McDougald Terrace, but they wanted to move closer to their mother. They both promised her that they were through with their drug habits. Laurence very quickly backslid on his promise, and Emma forced him out of her house. He returned to Durham. Tamara, however, was determined to turn over a new leaf. She joined a Narcotics Anonymous group in Wilson, and she quickly made friends with the recovering addicts.

> *She went faithfully to the meetings, she got herself a sponsor, and she even started going to conventions with her group there. One of*

the conventions was in Durham. My heart was beating so hard when she went there. I was so scared of what would happen when she was back in her old stomping ground. But she stayed with the convention, and she came back clean.

The group of friends she made was a source of strength to her as she struggled with her addiction.

They were together. They were each other's strength. If Tamara was having a hard time, someone would come to talk to her.

Tamara also found a boyfriend among the recovering addicts, a young man called Jason. There was a crucial difference between Tamara and Jason — a difference she was not at first aware of. While Tamara was in Narcotics Anonymous because she really wanted to get herself off drugs, Jason was there only because he had been ordered to attend by a judge.

If only she'd known more about him. She thought he was at the meetings because he believed in them. But then when his parole wound down he started missing the meetings. He was off his parole and he started getting high again.

One day, Jason came to Emma's house looking for Tamara. He needed money to buy drugs. Tamara was out, but Jason trashed her room, looking for something to pawn. He'd bought her a television, and he wanted it back. He'd already pawned his own Jeep.

Meanwhile, Emma's fears for her grandchildren were soon justified.

Those poor children. They used to talk about the strangest things when I visited them. They knew all about condoms, about sex, when they were still toddlers. They had so much sexual knowledge.

One day, Emma went to visit them from Wilson, and she took Bethany (who was four) and Tekeysia (five) to visit their older sister Chantoya, who was living with an aunt.

While we were out visiting, Keysia pulled on my sleeve and said, "Grandma, can I talk to you?" She told me about all the men coming and staying in the house and the behavior of her mom, and she said that she just couldn't stay there. So I went and talked to Anna, and she agreed to let me take Keysia back to Wilson with me.

After that, Bethany was left on her own with her mother and baby sister, and it wasn't long before Emma found herself going back and forth to Durham to take care of her vulnerable granddaughters. Eventually, Anna agreed to let Emma take Bethany too.

Then one night I got a phone call from a friend. Anna and her boyfriend were fighting, and Anna had just left her baby out in the street. Could I come as soon as possible to help? I called Sapphire's other grandmother and asked her to hold on to baby Sapphire. I woke up Tamara, and she got her boyfriend, and the three of us went down to Durham right away. We brought Sapphire back with us. So that's how I came to raise three of Anna's children.

Emma can't help judging her daughter for her poor parenting.

Nowadays I don't talk to her often. The way she's treated her children—she was not treated like that. I tried to provide my kids with mentors to get them out of the project. So when she had her kids I was shocked at how she treated them.

In 1998, Emma and her extended family returned to Durham. They had enjoyed living in Wilson, but Emma missed her childhood friends, and the whole family felt more of a sense of belonging in the city in which they had been raised. With their limited resources, they had trouble finding a suitable place to live. They moved several times in quick succession. At one point, they lived in a house divided into two apartments, and the upstairs was occupied by a troubled family. One day a fight broke out, a gun was fired, and a bullet came flying through the Johnston family's window. After that, the family moved twice more before finally finding a house in a relatively quiet cul-de-sac.

For Tamara, the move back to Durham proved disastrous. The problems didn't surface immediately. After their return, Tamara enrolled in a Narcotics Anonymous group in Durham and got herself a job at the VA hospital. She worked in the deli kitchen. Everyone knew and liked her. She kept the patients laughing.

She had a lot of friends here in Durham. But that's not what pulled her down. When Jason came walking down the street, that's when I knew she was doomed. His mother lived in Raleigh. I have no idea how he found out where we were. All I could say was "Lord have mercy!"

Emma told Jason that he was not allowed to set foot in her house. He answered with dark threats. He said that he would break in and hurt the people in the house. Emma locked all the doors and windows as securely as she could and waited for the worst to happen. Several times, Jason came to threaten the family and beat on the doors, and once Emma called the police to have him taken away. But after a while, her resistance seemed to be working. Jason stopped coming around to bother them.

But Tamara was still seeing him. Knowing that he couldn't visit her at her mother's house, she went to meet him at his workplace. He had taken a job in Durham so he could be close to Tamara, and she would visit him during his lunch break and after work. And the two of them used their time together to resume their life on drugs.

Before long Tamara was as addicted as she had ever been. Emma despaired that her daughter would ever recover from the disastrous relationship with this corrupting man.

One day, though, Jason failed to turn up for work. Everyone assumed that he had run off or gotten into trouble again with the police. Tamara knew he was living with his mother in Raleigh, but she had lost the phone number, so there was little she could do but wait for him to get in touch with her. He never did. Eventually another girlfriend of his called Emma's house. She was the mother of Jason's children, a rival in a sense, but she and Tamara had met and were fond of one another. She had found Emma's number in Jason's address book. Jason had been in a fight in his own neighborhood in Raleigh. He had been shot and killed.

Emma brought her grandchildren with her back to Durham, and shortly afterward the city's Social Services department told her that all three of them would be returned to their mother.

Anna put on a big act that she didn't drink anymore. She had more chances than anyone I ever seen.

But the new arrangement didn't last. It wasn't long before Social Services intervened to take the children away from Anna. Emma would have taken them back, but her own health was deteriorating rapidly. In 1998 Emma's doctor diagnosed her with congestive heart failure and refused to certify her to take care of her three grandchildren. As a result, all of Anna's children were moved to other families. Bethany was taken in by her biological father, Sammy. Chantoya remained with her aunt. Sapphire's father submitted the papers to adopt her to live with him — but just before she came to live with him he was shot and killed. So Sapphire and Tekeysia went into foster homes.

They were following their three younger brothers and sisters, who had been taken right out of the hospital. Emma was not able to save any of them from the disabling effects of the foster system.

My grandkids have been through so much; they need a lot of help. At first Sapphire had a wonderful foster home, but she did some bad things, and she had to move. Well, of course she doesn't behave normal. She feels a sense of abandonment. I warned my daughter, "You don't know what effect you're going to have on those children." The youngest, Seanna and Clarence, got taken by Social Services right away. But the older ones knew what it was to have a family, and to have it taken away from them. Even Seanna and Clarence, anytime you talk to them, they ask, "Have you seen our sisters?" They were very loving towards each other. They had to be because their mother was such an alcoholic. She was not a good, not a fair, not even an okay mother. It's all about her. "I've got a life and I've gotta live it." Well, when you have children you have to put your life on the back burner. Well, that is what it is.

But I believe God is always watching. When he punishes, it's just. It doesn't matter what you think. I pray a lot for my grandchildren, and for my kids. I love them no matter what they're doing. And I pray that God's will be done.

Chapter 5

The Hardest Trial

By the end of the millennium, Durham was becoming known nationally as an affordable, livable city for young professionals. The city had moved far beyond its core strengths in tobacco and education. In May 1988, *Out* magazine voted Durham one of the ten best cities in the United States for gays, citing its "atmosphere of tolerance usually associated with big cities." In the years that followed, both *Black Enterprise* and *Money* voted Durham the number-one place to retire in the United States. *BusinessWeek* voted it the number-three place in the United States to ride out a recession. *Fortune* ranked it number twelve for starting your own business. *Wired* magazine put it in the top ten "tech towns" in America.[1] The city began to develop a reputation not just as a place for economic opportunity, but also as a place for a distinctive lifestyle, based on appreciation of its southern roots combined with a new, youthful culture based on diversity, sophisticated taste, ecological sensitivity, and a global cultural outlook. As the tobacco factories and warehouses closed down, they were redeveloped as eclectic retail spaces or as stylish residential accommodations.

The city began developing a reputation for its food. Magnolia Grill, a restaurant with an original take on classic southern cuisine, was voted America's eleventh-best restaurant by *Gourmet* magazine.[2] The Durham Farmers' Market opened in 1998 and immediately became a treasured resource for local organically grown foods, handcrafted cheeses, and gourmet specialties. The city's growing population of Latino immigrants added to the diversity of food offerings, and by the end of the 2000s, food trucks were sprouting all over the city, breweries and specialty wine shops were opening up, and the downtown business district, which had been all but shuttered for the past three decades, began to develop as a showcase for new restaurants, wine bars, and fashionable pubs that were soon crowded with the city's young professional transplants. In 2010, *Bon Appetit* ranked Durham the "foodiest" small town in America. And on January 7, 2011, the *New York Times* included Durham as one of only four U.S. destinations in its list of "the 41 places to go in 2011." The paper cited particularly the "crop of standout restaurants and cafes" in the downtown business district.

Meanwhile, the city's reputation as a vibrant center for the arts continued to flourish and expand. The American Dance Festival, sponsored by Duke University, became a fixture on the international modern dance circuit, while the Full Frame Documentary Film Festival, also sponsored by Duke, quickly became one of the most vibrant film events in the country. In keeping with its reputation as a magnet for youth, Durham also became an increasingly significant center for the independent music industry, with a dozen record labels and several performance venues.

Durham's reputation grew alongside those of its partner cities, Chapel Hill, Carrboro, Cary and Raleigh. The Triangle area was increasingly recognized during the 2000s as one of the best places to live in the United States, with a golden combination of relatively low living costs; a vibrant, technology-intensive economy that proved itself highly resilient to economic downturns; an excellent cultural life; first-class medical facilities; and a highly educated population. What sets Durham apart from its neighbors is its ethnic diversity, which is perceived by many as emerging from its working-class roots. This is ironic. Durham has proven to be a magnet for ethnically diverse professionals who have added to the flair and charm of the city. But at the core of Durham's working-class roots is not diversity, but separation.

The only pall on Durham's reputation is its persistently high crime rate. For some, this is a reason to avoid Durham in favor of its neighbors Chapel Hill and Cary. But for others, the crime is part and parcel of Durham's diversity, its grittiness, its flavor of "real life" compared to the suburban sterility of its more staid neighbors. The city has done its best to minimize the threat, commenting in a newsletter that "public opinion polls last year [2007] indicated that by 8 to 1 Durham residents feel safe in their own community and that by 8 to 1 they feel safe in their own neighborhoods. Information and perceptions of Durham are often exaggerated by generalizing problems in parts of town to the community as a whole."[3] Indeed, the Durham police emphasized the concentration of crime in a few notorious areas when it launched "Operation Bull's Eye," a crime-prevention program that focuses on a two-square-mile area that accounts for a disproportionate share of Durham's violent crimes. As the police department's newsletter stated, "A spatial correlation [exists] between shots fired calls, violent gun crimes and validated gang members, and a disproportionate number in all three categories was located in a similar area of East Durham."[4] The area targeted by the police is overwhelmingly African American and includes on its periphery the neighborhoods where Emma and most of her family members live.

The truth is that Durham has become a great place to live provided you are not part of its minority underclass. As the city has burnished its reputation and drawn more and more affluent and highly educated residents, its black (and increasingly Latino) underclass has become more and more isolated and beleaguered. Parts of the city, including the McDougald public housing project and its surrounding neighborhoods, are virtually off limits for the city's middle-class residents. In recent years, parts of the downtown area have become magnets for upwardly mobile, successful people. Condos in remodeled warehouses and department stores are selling for a million dollars and more. And yet, just a block or two away in the streets of East Durham, houses are on the market for $20,000 and still can't find a buyer. The young black and Latino men hanging around on the street corners do not represent "diversity." They belong to another class altogether. As Durham's profile becomes more and more affluent, the gap between the trendy young pioneers and their invisible neighbors becomes more and more stark.

An alternative view of Durham was presented in the 2007 documentary film *Welcome 2 Durham*. The film takes a close look at the gang culture among young black males living in the housing projects and among the run-down neighborhoods of East Durham. The film mentions a number of high-profile black natives of Durham, including gospel singer Shirley Caesar, NBA stars Rodney Rogers and Ernie Barnes, NBA coach John Lucas, and entertainment lawyer Johnston Williams. As Williams comments, Durham is a town that has "black faces in high places."

And yet, in the past two decades, more and more young black men

East Durham Street scene. In spite of Durham's continued growth and prosperity, large parts of East Durham remain run down and beset by problems of poverty and violence (Simon Partner).

have been sucked into the gangs which began to move into Durham in the 1990s. As a prominent judge puts it, "If they don't have structure at home they will find it" in a gang. "This is my family," echoes a gang member, "me and my niggers." Back in the 1980s, Durham had a reputation as a slow town, nothing like the big cities with their brutal gang culture. But as one transplant who works for the city mortuary put it, "The scene over the years has gotten worser. I see them up here living. And I see them up there [in the mortuary] dead. I wished I woulda stayed in Baltimore."

In one chilling passage in the film, gang members show their gunshot wounds to the camera. Some of them are permanently crippled after being in the wrong place at the wrong time — and still they are the lucky ones. In another passage, gang members show off their guns. "I know thirteen-year-olds don't go nowhere without totes," says one. "Over on Holloway street, it's one side Bloods, the other side Crips. So you've got to have heat." An older gang member complains that the gun culture has gotten far beyond what he knew in his younger days. "We were trying to make money," he says. "But nowadays they're banging for nothing — because someone disrespects them."

Other voices in the film argue that the gangs themselves are not the problem. "Every one of us is in a gang," says one, "whether it's called a company or a church. Just because you're a member of the Bloods you're not automatically guilty." The gangs can offer a family life that is completely lacking at home for many of the young men. That could potentially be a positive role. But in too many cases their peers push them into destructive behavior.

The chances of a young black man making it on the streets of Durham are tragically low. In the late 1990s, between 70 and 90 children under age 18 were being treated annually for nonfatal gunshot wounds. Thirty or more young people were being murdered each year. The Youth Risk Behavior Survey of North Carolina estimated in 2000 that 15 percent of high school boys carried guns habitually for self-defense or aggression. Over 40 percent of middle school boys had carried a weapon at least one time in the past year, and in 50 percent of cases that weapon was a gun. Durham had a very high percentage of children in Department of Social Services custody: nine children out of every thousand. Moreover, in any given semester more than 12 percent of middle and high school students — almost all of them black — were suspended for disciplinary problems. Around 50 percent of black male high school students dropped out before completing their schooling. Only 50 percent of elementary and middle school students were performing at their grade level. The lowest-performing schools were in the predominantly black neighborhoods. Worst of all was Emma's old school, Pearson. Only 20 percent of children were performing at their grade level.[5]

A 2006 study of young black men nationwide found that even in a good economy, almost 20 percent were unemployed — a far higher percentage than for any other ethnic group. Only 7.5 percent had graduated from college — the lowest percentage for any ethnic group except Latinos. Only 77 percent had graduated from high school. Young African Americans made less money than whites at every level of education. One in ten young black men was in prison. While African American men rep-

resented only 14 percent of the population of young men in the United
States, they represented over 40 percent of the prison population. Thirty-
eight percent of young black men lacked health insurance, and young
black men were almost twice as likely to die as young white men — the
leading causes being homicide, suicide, and accident. Young black men
were seventeen times more likely to die in a homicide than young white
men.[6] This was the environment in which Emma's younger children,
and then her grandchildren, grew up.

In July 2000, Emma turned fifty. She was already grandmother to
more than a dozen children, the oldest of whom were well into their
teens. She had experienced a lifetime of turmoil, abuse, addiction, chaos,
and discrimination. In an ideal world, Emma should have been able to
retire quietly from life's upheavals and live out her days in peace. But
Emma's greatest tragedy still remained in the future.

In early 2001, Emma and Jimmy found a small, neat house on a
quiet backstreet. After so many years of bringing up children and grandchildren and caring for sick and disabled family members, Emma now
found herself in an empty nest. Laurence had found a job in Greensboro,
Benjamin had moved in with his girlfriend, and Michael was renting an
apartment so that he, too, could be more independent.

Emma's life with Jimmy should have been good. Jimmy was everything that Emma could want in a husband — caring, loyal, gentle, and
kind. But for the last decade and more, the two of them have been apart
more than they have been together. Jimmy had been living in Oxford,
about thirty miles from Durham, before he met Emma, and he has kept
his home there. He escapes to Oxford when he finds his marriage oppres-
sive. Emma blames herself.

> *He just couldn't cope with my bossiness. He went out of his way to
> accommodate me when he came into my life. But I started treating
> him like I did my own children. Jimmy has never drawn his hand
> back to strike me. He's never abused me. In fact that's one reason
> that he paid so much attention to me — he didn't like the abuse I'd
> been putting up with all of my life. But by the time I met Jimmy I
> had myself become abusive. He took it from me for years. My close
> friend came and said bad things to him, and I allowed it. Jimmy felt*

*disrespected. He said, "You can care about someone, but you have to
care about yourself too." I abused him verbally, and verbal abuse can
be worse than physical. Words can cut like a knife. Once words are
out, you can't take them back. I did it in front of the children too.
He was working hard for my family. I realize where I went wrong,
but I can't undo it now.*

Emma has had cause for deep self-reflection in many areas of her
life.

*I wished many times that I had made different choices. Sometimes
I even wished that I was someone else. No matter who we are, or
what our background, sooner or later we must bear the consequences
of our actions. Each of us can only work with what we have in us.
But when children make grown-up choices, everyone suffers.*

Recently, Emma watched a documentary on fetal alcohol syndrome.
It was the first time she was forced to confront the possibility of her own
responsibility for some of the difficulties faced by her children.

*I drank when I was pregnant with all of my children, except
Michael. I didn't know alcohol was a drug. I smoked a lot too. I
didn't know that was considered harmful to a fetus. Today, with
Anna drinking the way she does, I can't help believing there's a connection. A few weeks ago, Anna came out of the blue. She was acting
all strange, as though she'd just come out of a mental hospital. She
was talking so slow. I don't know. Lord, please forgive me if I've
messed these people up. At the time I didn't know. But now I wonder.*

In July, 2001, something very unexpected and special happened to
Emma. She acquired a public voice. The previous month she had been
taking a computing course at the Salvation Army, taught by a volunteer
from the Durham Literacy Center. In addition to computing, the teacher
was also helping students with their GED certification. Emma had passed
her GED when she was in her twenties, so she spent the time writing on
her own. One day, the teacher asked Emma what she was writing about.

*I said, "Just life." He read what I'd written and said, "Do you
have any more?" And I showed him my notebook with more of my
writing. He asked me if I'd mind him showing it to a friend of his,*

and I said, "Sure." A while later I got a call. The man said he was the editor of the Herald-Sun *newspaper. He had seen my writing and he liked it. "You write about stuff that you know," he said. "You don't stereotype people like some writers do." He wanted me to write more. I told him I'd be happy to, but that if I write, I'm going to tell it like it really is. I'm going to write that we poor people want as much for our children as wealthy people do. Just because we're poor, we still want our children to succeed. He said that he would like me to write just that. And in the meantime he was going to publish the piece my teacher had shown him.*

Emma did indeed tell it like it was. Her first published piece told of her disappointment with the Durham police force, which in her opinion showed a lack of concern toward poor black residents of Durham. She blamed the police for the death of her brother Junebug, and she gave other examples of the police devaluing the needs of poor black citizens. As Emma put it, "We feel that as a viable segment of this community, we should be able to count on the same courteous, timely service given to the rest of this society no matter where we live."

After that, Emma began contributing regularly to the *Herald-Sun*. In the early 2000s, she was writing an article every two to three weeks. For the most part, she wrote about the troubles that had shadowed her own life.

If only one person can read about how I live and the lessons I learn on a daily basis (and realize that someone like me can live joyously off a fixed income), then I have accomplished something important.

Many of Emma's articles were deeply spiritual. She wanted to share the spiritual wisdom she had earned through the harsh experiences of her life.

The most precious gifts we can be given are grace and mercy. I have heard at different times in my life that diamonds are a girl's best friend. Some men think that being given a powerful car is the ultimate gift they could ever receive. But we have gifts of a spiritual nature waiting for us before we ever reached this Earth, and they have a value that cannot be measured.

160

Some people crave power and do whatever is deemed necessary to achieve it. Faith in God is so powerful that it cannot be measured. As long as we have it and activate it, we are covered by the blood of our Savior, the Lord Jesus Christ. Oh, what a precious gift this is.

Many of us have problems with substance abuse. The Lord gave man the knowledge and creativity to bring about tools to help us overcome, reach back and help others achieve the victory over this powerful enemy. Tell me, can we think of any gift, of any amount that would measure up to the gifts given to us by our Savior?

Another exquisite gift we have been given is love. Love is infectious, spreading from one person to another — loving, giving, influencing and blessing one another through the Lord. Imagine, God is love. Think about the love he has shown to us by giving his only son as a sacrifice for a sinful world so we would have the choice to have everlasting life.

There are so many of us living below the poverty line, but the Lord has seen fit to provide us with our needs on a daily basis.

Shortly after she started writing, the September 11 tragedy transfixed the American people. Emma was shocked like the rest of the nation. But the disaster also brought out a darker, more critical side of her worldview.

The tragedy that struck our nation brought Americans together in a way no event that I know of ever has, as should be, but there is a group of people in isolation that really don't know where they really fit. They have been treated as outsiders all of their lives, yet they are well aware that this country was built off of the sweat and tears of their people, and in some families people are still struggling to survive. Durham has a lot of work to do as a city, community and as a society. We have whole communities that feel as if their plight doesn't matter and never has. There is a feeling of exclusion instead of inclusion. People who have felt dehumanized for so long must have their feelings validated. Some wonder what use is there in trying when they are already out of the game. Please, let's take a closer look at home. We should do everything we can to help the victims of the outrageous attack on us, but we must not forget mending starts at home.

If we realize this as a nation, maybe terrorists won't have so many gaps and cracks to slip through.

A theme that Emma wrote on frequently was the dangers that black children faced growing up in poor communities, surrounded by the temptations of twenty-first-century culture.

Our children learn by example, so we must show them that doing the right thing alienates us from others sometimes. As time goes on, there will be rewards for doing what you know is right. Rewards come in all kinds of forms, sometimes it is monetary, recognition or just a wonderful feeling that comes with the power of the spirit. When one lives in an environment where the elements penetrate our homes whether we want them to or not— the loud music, vulgar language, people selling crack right out in public— and calling the police does not bring satisfactory results, these are a few of Purgatory's weapons that we must fight against if we want safe and secure homes. Children are born loving us unconditionally. They have no concept of substance abuse, money problems, careers or any of the excuses we use to push them aside. Children still love us when we neglect and abuse them. Their deepest desire is for us to pay a little attention to them. When we show a little affection, the love is renewed all over again.

Emma had no hesitation in blaming parents, and there was a strong element of bitterness in her thoughts as she wrote these articles. Emma prided herself that her own children had never gone hungry or ill clothed. But she had known so much of this sort of abuse in her own family!

Some children are hungry, not because there is no money to buy food, but because mommy used the food stamps to buy drugs. Some children do not have decent clothes and shoes, not because the parents didn't receive the money to buy them, but because the parents used the money to throw an alcohol and drug party. These kinds of behaviors are some of the reasons the social workers in protection and foster care face a crowded and growing client list. Years ago, when a family was identified as needing help, usually it was because one or both caregivers were in an accident, had a serious illness or were mentally unstable. It was very rare to see or hear of neglect or abuse happening in the community. But we are now in a war with substance abuse and the casualty rate is very high. Not only are the caregivers of these children being destroyed, the lives of their children are threatened. When our actions damage the lives of a four- or five-year-old child, then I think we owe an explanation to someone of authority. We do not have the right to destroy these young lives.

In another article, Emma wrote,

There are so many caught like fish in a net, trapped and not knowing how to get free. There are a thousand reasons why a person may try drugs: to fit in with others, to see what it's like and so on. Once a person becomes addicted, the drug is in control, not the user. It affects not only the user, but everyone connected to them. The person's whole personality changes. I believe it takes away their basic morals and values and replaces them with lies, disrespect, manipulation and other qualities needed to live the life of an addict. I know all too well about this, because several members of my family live this lifestyle today. At first, I tried to change them, and I was disappointed and hurt at every turn. I learned some tough lessons the hard way.

Emma understood that these problems were directly linked to issues of race:

After slavery, the civil rights movement, fighting for one basic dignity at a time and so many of us dying for the smallest infraction, from individuals and organized groups like the Ku Klux Klan, we still held on. Now we have to be afraid of our own people robbing and killing each other. Mothers and fathers in many households have replaced their children's welfare with alcohol and drugs. So many see their parents and friends getting high that it becomes a part of their everyday world.

Nor did she hesitate to take her share of the blame in this.

I know as the mother of nine children, that if I had it to do over, the difference in what I did and what I would do would be a world apart. Children imitate their environment and what they see. If they see people getting high regularly, most likely they will end up involved in that behavior.

Emma's own children and grandchildren have been living witness to the truth of her words. Through the past decade, her children have remained Emma's joy, her life, and also her agony and her trial.

Ironically, though, it was not her problem children who were to cause Emma the greatest suffering of her hard life. It was her pride and joy, her youngest child, Michael.

Michael had never given Emma any trouble. He returned from Wilson with less than a year to go of high school, but his heart had never been in his studies, and once back in Durham, he did not reenroll. Instead, he went to work as a server at a local Pizza Hut. He knew that his mother was hard-pressed financially, and he wanted to be independent. A little later, he fell in love with the sister of his best friend. Michael moved into a small apartment, and Vondra moved in with him.

Michael had a mentor, an Episcopal priest called Father Franklyn Johnson. Michael formed a close relationship with Father Franklyn, helping him at his home and church, and staying with him and helping out on his alpaca ranch in rural North Carolina, and at his country home in upstate New York. Once, Emma went to visit him on the ranch.

> When I saw one of those alpacas, I was so scared I didn't know what to do. Michael cracked his sides. "Mama, I didn't even know you could run," he laughed.

Emma has a photo of Michael on her wall. He is at Father Franklyn's house in upstate New York, standing in the middle of a hay field, smiling happily. Living with his girlfriend, seeing his family every day, spending time with his close friends, helping his mother when he could, he lived without any thought that violence and death might be closing in on him. He drank only moderately and did not take drugs.

> His was a laid-back personality. He was hard to anger. Some of my other children, they'd flip out, but Michael could always talk about things. He was easy to forgive. I thought it was amazing. If it's over with, it's over with. Once he'd put it behind him, he wouldn't talk about it or bring it up. I compare that with myself— it's a trait that I wish I had.

He lived for his family. He came by at least once a day to visit his mother, and he was adored by all of his nieces and nephews. Nor was he always easy on them. Michael was intensely aware of the dangers faced by a teenage girl in East Durham. He would insist on meeting their boyfriends, and he would not hesitate to warn the girls against a boy he considered unsuitable.

Out of all their uncles it was Michael they loved. They just loved him to death. He was a hard taskmaster when they were seeing older boys. He'd march them home, or he'd march them to me. When they started to date a boy, it was Michael that they first brought him to meet. And he'd say, "You need to have her home by ten!" You'd think he was their daddy! Tekeysia would tell the boy, "That's my uncle, and that's just the way he acts."

Michael was close to his brothers, particularly his nearest brother, Benjamin. And he was intensely loyal to his girlfriend and companion, Vondra. To the rest of the world, Michael was polite and respectful. But he kept his distance. His greatest attachment of all was to his mother.

Michael acted less than his twenty-five years. He came to visit me very often, and he called several times a day. He wanted to know if I needed anything, was I eating? I had to go to the hospital once, and while I was there they couldn't get him out. He slept there. He thought I was going to pass. All of my kids care about me, and they'll call up to check up on me. But Michael was much closer. I can't say he was more concerned than they were; he just showed it more. The others, once they talked to me on the phone, they'd know that I was all right. But Michael would always come in person, even if it was just for a few minutes. He'd come just about every day. And I could always put my finger on him if I was trying to find him — he made a habit of telling me where he was.

On Emma's street there lived a small child called Lewis. He was the son of a drug-addicted mother who had virtually abandoned him to the care of her neighbors. Michael was only too happy to help take care of the little boy. Lewis was not related to Michael in any way, but when Michael saw him suffering from neglect, he became the baby's father in all but name.

That little boy, he called me grandma because he didn't know any better. They were all taking Lewis in, up and down the street. All of us were crazy about him. One time, Michael went out to the store to buy Pampers for the child. He would do that sort of thing; he was always spending his money on someone else. Well, Father Franklyn sees him in the store buying Pampers, and before I know it his wife calls me up. "Emma," she says, "is there something you haven't been telling us?" They thought Michael had a baby he was keeping secret from them!

Michael was not a part of the pervasive gang culture in Durham, nor was he involved in drugs, alcohol, or violence. But the culture of violence was all around him. For an African American youth in East Durham, it is hard to isolate oneself from the gangs. A short time before his death, Michael got a warning that some gang members had their eye on him. One day, late in July, he was staying overnight at the apartment of Vondra's best friend when there was a violent banging on the door. Someone was trying to kick their way into the apartment. Michael and the others stayed quiet, and the intruder eventually left, but Emma took the incident as an omen.

Do the math, child. You're the only one there that was out of place. You're the only one with no family or friends living there. And they try and break in the door while you're there. I told him right there, I said, "Please don't go back out there." I just knew that night that he went again. All that night I just couldn't sleep.

At the beginning of August 2007, Michael went again to visit his girlfriend at her friend's apartment in Mangum Square.

He never came back.

At some point on that evening, Michael was accosted by fifteen or more attackers, beaten and kicked, and left for dead. His attackers were leaving the scene when some of them noticed him moving. They went back and shot Michael five times. He was found by police in the Mangum Square parking lot and taken to Duke University Hospital, where he was declared dead a short time later.

A few days after the murder, someone left Michael's wallet in his mother's mailbox. It still had all of his credit cards in it, as well as his ID card.

Two men were arrested in the murder of Michael Johnston. One of them was tried and found guilty of Michael's murder. He was sentenced to twenty-three years in the state penitentiary. At the time of the murder he had been on probation after a drug conviction, but because of personnel problems in the Durham probation office, he was not under active supervision. He made a plea deal in exchange for testifying against his accomplice. But at the trial he went back on the deal, and the second defendant was acquitted.

> *Murder is in a unique category of death. There is no time to anticipate. It is the unlawful killing of one human by another, according to the dictionary. But actually murder kills a part of all who loved the victim. Hearts shatter like glass. The heartache never ends.*

Michael's funeral service was held at St. Titus Episcopal Church. One after another, Michael's family members and friends testified to his sweet and gentle nature. The church was packed with friends, family, and well-wishers. Particularly notable were the large numbers of children, in the pews and on the floor. When the time came to close the casket, one of the children tried to hold it open, shouting, "Don't you shut him up in there!"

> *Michael had a sweet soul and it came out. It was an aura that people could feel. They would tell me, "Michael is something else." And I would say to myself, "So I'm not the only one that noticed that." Naturally as his mother I saw the best in him. Of course he made mistakes, but when it came to older people, no one ever came to me and said that Michael had talked back to them. When they called him, he came. And if he didn't like what they said, then he held his peace.*

Emma found an outlet in her writing. In the *Herald-Sun*, she published a series of articles about violence in Durham's black community and the devastation it created.

> *The murder of my beloved son changed me. It heightened my awareness of the shape our community is in and which way it is going. It is a shame it took the taking of my child to see what was really happening around me. We see crime being committed, but we*

look the other way. We complain about the police but do nothing to improve our relationship with them. No one is immune to the negative vibrations spreading from illegal activities. Love is a powerful emotion, but so is hate.

In spite of her grief and bitterness at Michael's death, Emma did not lose her faith.

Sometimes Jesus calls his angels home. People wonder why in the world God took their loved one and left someone else that's doing evil acts and hurting people. But God has his reasons whenever he does something like that. I believe that Michael is watching over me. He may not have an earthly body, but he has a spiritual body. While we're living we have a life force, a spirit in us that you can easily see. We all to have to leave these earthly bodies. Only our spirit survives. I hope that Michael is still learning wherever he is. I do not want him to go into the lake of fire.

The one positive outcome of the tragedy and trauma of Michael's death has been Emma's connection with the community working to reduce violence in Durham and offer comfort to its victims. When she was at her lowest ebb, Emma met Marcia Owen, founder of the Religious Coalition for a Nonviolent Durham. Marcia is an inspiring figure, a middle-class white woman who has devoted her life to the underprivileged victims of violence, and to the young people who are most at risk. Recognizing Emma's intelligence and articulacy, Marcia quickly recruited her to help with the coalition's activities, and Emma soon became a core member. Emma also joined the Durham chapter of Parents of Murdered Children, a group that offers mutual support and that holds annual memorials for the ever-growing toll of murder victims.

In a typical year, Durham suffers twenty-five or more homicides — a little below the peak in the late 1990s, but still tragically high for a city Durham's size. The majority take place in the African American neighborhoods of East Durham, and most of the victims are young black men. Each year, fifty or more parents and dozens of brothers and sisters are left grief stricken and dazed at the senseless loss of a person they love. Year after year, the toll of suffering mounts. There are literally hundreds of bereft families, many of them almost invisible, feeling that no one cares, that the death of a young black man is seen by the community as a routine event meriting little more than a few lines in the local newspaper. When a white student was murdered in Chapel Hill in 2008, thousands of students and residents honored her in an outpouring of public grief. By contrast, the memorial vigils that the Religious Coalition holds for murdered black men and women are sometimes attended by no more than a handful of people.

Emma felt bitterly this belittling and denial of the worth of her son. In spite of her repeated requests, the district attorney dragged his feet over the investigation of the suspects in her son's death. In Emma's view, he ignored important information that she provided to him. She felt that the police were less than thorough in their investigation. From their point of view, Michael was just another victim in a cycle of violence that was so ingrained in the life of the city that it had become part of the routine. As a poor black woman on disability, she felt powerless to influence the course of events or to make her voice heard.

After the tragedy of her son's loss, Emma has had to move on with her life. Her remaining children and grandchildren need her support, and even though Emma has no financial resources and little physical strength, she has been called on to stand by her family members as they endure one trial after another.

None of Emma's children has succeeded in breaking into the ranks of the growing middle class. Emma's two eldest, Donna and Jake, have been the steadiest. Both finished high school, and both have held steady employment throughout their working lives. Donna is now in the process of buying a house, a first for any member of Emma's family. Jake has held down two jobs for more than twenty years, both on cleaning crews for industrial facilities. Although he has remained affectionate to his mother, there has always been a distance between them since Jake was moved to another family as a small child. A number of years ago, he became a Muslim Rastafarian and changed his name to Abdul Rahim. After divorcing his first wife, he married again fifteen years ago, to a woman several years older than himself. Emma has never met his second wife. Jake has raised two children — one his own and one the child of his first wife — and recently became a grandfather, but Emma hardly knows his children.

Donna never married, but she had four children by two different fathers: Serena and Sylvester, Ronnie and Desiree. Desiree has been in constant trouble throughout her life, often on the run from the police, and with several jail sentences on her record. She has a son, one of Donna's four grandchildren, who now lives with Donna.

Emma's middle children all continue to live with severe problems. Laurence, Tamara, Brianna and Anna have all been diagnosed with mental illness — which Emma blames on drug and alcohol addiction. Laurence, Tamara and Brianna have been in and out of treatment programs. Brianna completed a course in culinary arts and went on to enroll in a cosmetology program in Kentucky, but in spite of her skills, her drug and health problems have prevented her from ever settling down to a steady job.

Laurence's programs of treatment included rehabilitation and outright hospitalization.

> *The drugs put him in a battle trying to get straight again. He was like a baby learning to walk. He didn't have to take it but one time. It's turned him and his sister Brianna's lives upside down. When things were at their worst, both Laurence and Brianna attempted suicide. Those children have so much to offer. Brianna is a culinary artist. She does people's hair so that their friends think they've been to a beauty salon. She does her nails with beautiful designs — people always want to know where she had it done. She sews stuff. She draws wonderful pictures. And Laurence made beautiful old-fashioned pottery. One lady offered him $150 for a pitcher he had made. They could have accomplished so much. That stuff stole their lives.*

Emma's children have been making steady progress in reclaiming their lives. Brianna continues to take classes to help her adjust to a drug-free life, and she attends Narcotics Anonymous meetings. Laurence has been off drugs for some time and is living independently in Greensboro, where he has held a steady job for the past nine years. But he suffers from chronic mental and physical problems, including high blood pressure, back pain, and heart disease.

Laurence's move to Greensboro is frustrating for Emma in many ways. She has no long-distance phone service, and she has to rely on Laurence to call her. He is very caring and worries about her health. But she worries about him too and gets anxious when she can't easily contact him. Laurence is supposed to be going to a clinic to have his heart evaluated, but she's afraid he will be too scared of the outcome to go through with the checkup.

On the other hand, though, she recognizes that the move has been good for him.

Durham is the place where the bad stuff is. It's not just my children. I have friends; they get high here in Durham. They'll go somewhere else, and when I see them they'll look so much better. But when they come back here, it's the same as before. I don't know what it is about Durham. If you grew up or were raised here, you need to stay away if you ever want to get off that stuff.

Laurence has a girlfriend in Greensboro. She is the first steady girlfriend he has had. She knows little about his past or the difficulties he has encountered, and Emma is praying that the relationship will last.

Laurence is a wonderful child as far as I am concerned. He's always concerned about me, about my health. He's always there for me, even though he resides in another city. We're very close friends as well as mother and son. I know it's selfish, but I would like it if he was around a bit more. I want Laurence to know I appreciate him. But I don't want him to get into any avoidable situations.

Tamara has continued to struggle with drug addiction. She has had a steady boyfriend for many years. Freddie has been a support to her, but he has also contributed to her continuing problems with addiction. Tamara continues to struggle also with mental illness.

I blame it on crack. None of them had problems when they were born or when they were in elementary school. They went to the doctor regularly — even as a poor black woman, I made sure that they were properly cared for. I think the crack did something to them. Four of my children are taking medications for mental problems. Their addiction did something to their brains — it destabilized them.

171

Unlike her sisters, Tamara did not have children. Once she became pregnant but suffered a late-stage miscarriage. Then, in 2010, Tamara became pregnant again at the age of forty. She was considered high risk due to her age, and she had been doing her best to take things carefully. But in March 2011, on her way back from a visit to her mother, she was struck by a car and her leg was broken in three places. The fetus survived that accident, but two months later Tamara suffered the tragedy of a stillbirth.

Brianna's life has been as chaotic as those of her siblings. Her drug addiction and her amazing gifts of persuasion have proven to be a dangerous combination. Over the years she has antagonized her entire community by sweet-talking people into lending her drugs or money and never repaying them. She has been severely beaten several times, almost losing the sight in one eye. Once she was found, naked and severely beaten, lying in a gutter in Durham's West End. A witness who called the police said he thought the men were kicking a dog.

> She can't show her face anywhere in public, she got so many enemies. And it's not just in Durham. She can't go to Oxford or Henderson either. She got beat up so bad up in Henderson that when I went to see her in the hospital, I passed right by her. Her face was twice as big as usual. And she had bruises all over her back. She even got into trouble in Wilson. She visited me there one time and she got people there giving her money. She talked the lady who lived right next door to me out of her money.

In recent years, Brianna has lived with a boyfriend in an apartment in the West End district of Durham. Her boyfriend has many problems of his own, including mental disabilities and a range of physical ailments.

> Brianna went on his behalf to Social Services. She made him go to the dentist when his teeth got rotten. She took him to the doctor and makes sure he goes back to get his medicines. She is drawn to needy people. She is good at taking care of them. She has the best heart ... until those urges come.

In spite of her many talents, Brianna has never held down a job. She is on a wide array of medicines for various mental and physical health problems. They tend to make her drowsy, and she often sleeps for much of the day.

> *She's so talented. She draws, she paints, she cooks, she does hair. But her mind doesn't function too good.*

Brianna's children have also had troubled lives, and Emma worries about them, particularly young Lavaughan. Lavaughan was raised by a family friend, Ms. Spence. A gifted child, he graduated from Hillside High School and has excellent prospects to get a college degree. But Emma is deeply worried about him.

> *That boy is running around with a crew of killers. I told him, "They will hurt you. Suppose they told you to hurt someone in your family." And he said, "I gotta do what I gotta do, or they're going to hurt me."*
>
> *I love that boy so much because he spent so much time with me when I was by myself. He's the one grandchild who'd come. We'd talk till two or three in the morning. It hurts to see him in danger. I tried to do something. But everyone said he can't just walk away. You don't just quit the "boys' club."*
>
> *If he stays with them, he's just as much of a menace as they are. When he's with them he does what they do. To some innocent person. Sometimes when you want to join, they give you a "task." That's what my son Michael's life was worth. They killed him so they could join the Bloods.*
>
> *Everyone wants to help him, but he won't be helped. So I gave it to God.*

Anna has been the most troubled of all of Emma's children. Like her siblings, Anna has suffered from addiction for all of her adult life. But her drug of choice is alcohol. After having seven children by seven different fathers, Anna continued to live a wild life of sex and drinking. Her mental problems have left her severely impaired. She is subject to blackouts and has been found wandering naked around the streets of McDougald Terrace, where she lives. When she is having a bad spell, she is barely able to take care of herself. She has had no space in her life for her children, most of whom have been completely separated from her.

When they have spent time with her, though, her influence has been poisonous. Inevitably, they have grown up troubled.

Sapphire has been through a total of four foster homes. Her younger brother, Clarence, has been more fortunate. He was adopted as a baby by a woman whose sister happened to be a friend of Emma's.

My friend Doris, she came looking for me one day and she said, "You know my sister's got your daughter's baby. She's crazy about that baby."

Because of this connection, Emma has been able to keep in closer touch with Clarence than with others of her grandchildren. Her friend shows her pictures of him, and Emma has even been allowed to visit him a few times.

Emma's youngest surviving child, Benjamin, has also been a cause of worry, though much less so than Emma's other children.

Benjamin was a bright, creative child. He was popular, and he stayed out of trouble. He was also very good at sports and won a dozen trophies that still sit in Emma's living room.

But Benjamin was also a master of deceit.

He'd go to the store, and if he saw someone he knew he'd tell them it was his birthday, so they'd give him money. Then eventually they'd come to me and say, "When is his birthday? I done gave him money twice!" I punished him for that, but he continued to do it and they continued to give him money.

Benjamin also got money by scoring for the teams in neighborhood sports. Although he grew up short, he was muscular and athletic, and he was always an asset to his team. The local drug pushers would often give rewards to the boys who played especially well, and Benjamin added to his income in this way.

Benjamin continued to do well in school all the way through the twelfth grade. Throughout his teen years, he looked so small and childlike that he was easily able to ride the buses on a child's fare. But in twelfth grade, Benjamin found a girlfriend and dropped out of school. The girl, whose name was Andrea, had two children and was a student at Durham Tech. She gave Benjamin a key to her apartment, which was on the same street as Emma's, and instead of going to school, Benjamin began hanging out at her place. Emma didn't even know her son had dropped out until her friend told her that Benjamin was going in and out of Andrea's apartment.

Benjamin's girlfriend kept him for almost five years. In all that time he did very little except play video games in her apartment, but somehow he charmed her into supporting him financially. In fact, Benjamin has avoided work for most of his adult life. For a while he went to work for his stepfather Jimmy, but Jimmy had to pick him up and personally accompany him to the job every day — or he would never show up.

It wasn't until Benjamin had a child of his own, with his current girlfriend Devon, that he began to face up to his responsibilities. Benjamin adores his baby, whose name is Alisha, and for two years he was the primary caregiver while Devon went out to work. For a while he went out to work to help support the family that he's so proud of. But then he got arrested for drug dealing and spent time in jail.

Emma continues to have a strained relationship with her son. She is constantly frustrated by his laziness and lack of drive.

A few years back, Benjamin got into some trouble because a friend of his got a driver's license in Benjamin's name. Benjamin doesn't even drive—none of my children except Laurence and Tamara do. But this friend got some citations on the license. So Jimmy decides to help Benjamin clean all that up, get it off his record. I have a friend at Legal Aid, and they have a class there to teach you how to expunge strikes off your name. After he completed the class they would give him a voucher and he would take it to the courthouse—and his record would be cleared. I made the appointment for him and they called to remind him, so he was well aware. But he didn't even go. I blame myself too. I let him stay for years after he should have been out in the world. It did him more harm than good.

After all her trials, Emma now lives alone in her small but comfortable house. Her home is the center for family celebrations, and for consultations about the many difficulties that continue to afflict her family.

Emma and Jimmy remain married. Jimmy continues to live between Oxford and Durham. He remains independent, but he always checks up on Emma and makes sure that she is taking her medicines for diabetes and congestive heart failure.

He helps me with the big jobs that I can't do myself. I don't have a lawn mower; he's always come and kept the lawn for me. He rakes the leaves. And if I'm sick then he'll care for me, no matter what.

Unfortunately, Emma is sick much more of the time than she would like. She suffers from a wide range of ailments, any one of which might flare up and disable her for days or weeks. Her diabetes requires constant management, which is made difficult by her money problems. Often at the end of the month she has no money to buy food, and she has to scrimp and make do with whatever is left in the fridge. When she skips meals, her blood sugar can become very hard to control. Emma's heart is struggling to keep going, all the more so because of her very substantial weight gain in recent years. Emma struggles to her feet at the best of times, and she cannot walk far without the aid of a walker. Her heart problems often cause her ankles to swell up, and when that happens she has no choice but to remain lying down with her legs up. Emma also suffers from gout, asthma, emphysema, arthritis, and kidney disease. To battle these ailments she takes a formidable array of drugs every day. And many days she is forced to take powerful painkillers that leave her drowsy and addled for much of the time. She has no car and is dependent on the kindness of others to get out of her house. Often her friend Marcia will pick her up and take her to a community event or just to the grocery store. But there are weeks that go by without Emma ever leaving the house.

She continues to struggle with severe poverty. Her family has many financial needs, and if Emma had any surplus she could be sure that they would come to beg some of it from her. But more often than not she's unable to help them. Her welfare check of $674 barely stretches over her own monthly expenses. After rent and utilities (which can be more than $200 in winter), television ($60), telephone ($50) and insurance ($60), Emma is left with barely enough for food. She often runs out toward the end of the month and is forced to rely on local charities to deliver her supplies for the remaining days.

Still, Emma has her friends, and she remains at the center of a family that, for all its problems, does not lack for love and togetherness. Emma is on the phone much of the day with friends and family, and Jimmy is often there to help her and keep her company. Emma remembers to count her blessings each day, and indeed she is grateful to her creator for the benefits she still has.

When Emma looks back on her life, one of her big regrets is never having worked.

It's a part of my life I really missed. I don't know exactly what I've got a passion for, but I have one for something. It's so frustrating.

Her biggest worry remains her grandchildren.

At one time, our elders looked forward to retirement and made plans to go on a cruise, drive across the country or visit relatives they have not seen in many years. Instead, they are getting children off to school, washing clothes, giving baths and cooking dinner every night. The twilight years don't seem so golden now because so many of us already in our twilight years are still doing what we did 20 years ago. And this time, it's much harder. Still, the most important ingredient for our grandchildren is unconditional love, then food and water, plus our day-to-day care. Unfortunately, some of these children do not have the nurturing on a day-to-day basis. Many times this is where grandparents or older relatives step in. Even though many have raised children, starting over is harder. Some do not have the stamina, some have health problems and others just plain don't have the patience they once had. Their nerves, many times, are stretched to the limit. The majority of older people have some form of high blood pressure, diabetes, heart disease, arthritis or some other ailments that come with age. So many times, when taking on the children we also take on the parents and whatever problems they have. That can be taxing as well.

As Emma's own health has declined, she has had to confront the untimely deaths of many of her close friends.

Nookie, who for years was Emma's chief drinking partner, was one of the first. She felt ill one day and went to the hospital. The doctors couldn't find anything wrong with her and sent her home. When Emma went to visit her later that day, she found an ambulance at the home. Nookie died later that night. No one knows what caused her death.

Then there was Jodie, also a member of their drinking group. She died of an overdose. None of the group even knew that she was using drugs. But her son was a pusher and he supplied his own mother with the drugs that killed her.

Then there was Martha-Kay, also a member of Emma's inner circle. She called Emma one day and said that she was coming over for a drink. But she never arrived. She was found later, collapsed on the stairs in her house.

There were other deaths too — friends who died of overdoses, friends who were run down, friends who were shot, and one close relative who drowned in Jordan Lake. Death, including death by violence, has always been a presence haunting Emma's life. As the years draw in, death seems to loom larger and darker.

Nowadays, Emma has plenty of time to reflect on her life. On the whole, she remains remarkably positive in spite of all the difficult experiences in her past and the health, family, and financial problems that she continues to face.

I believe that everybody has to go through something. Unfortunately, I went through a lot of things — molestation, rape, all these things where I was not able to help myself. But that is not so uncommon today. To me, this book — the story of my life — is a testimony to the resilience of my mother.

She took on the challenge of raising siblings when they were orphaned early. She raised my brothers and me even though she was illiterate. When I broke her heart by getting pregnant at thirteen, she didn't turn her face away from me. She opened her arms with love. I was most fortunate in having that parent. I thank God for giving her to me.

And I was fortunate to be able to become a published writer. I never thought I'd be in a position to have anything published or read, something that people would read and have opinions about, even though I was put out of school in junior high. I never took a journalism class. I never even imagined that someone would take something that I wrote and would think it was important enough to publish in a newspaper. That was a miracle.

And then, I was very fortunate to be put in a position to meet special people. When I was in McDougald Terrace, I had a special friend who encouraged the faith that I had. I had these faithful feelings but didn't know what to do with them. She talked to me; she encouraged my faith in the Lord. It just grew into me. It made me stronger, so much stronger. Just recently she told me that she always knew that God had favor over me.

Then, after the death of my son, when the Religious Coalition reached out to me, I met Marcia Owen and so many others. I could not believe that I was in the midst of so many people with views about things I knew nothing about. I couldn't believe that there are people who just love you because they believe in love.

I have always believed that faith and works go hand in hand. My faith has brought me through times that were so good I almost couldn't believe in the blessings Jesus has given me. On the other end, events have been so tragic that if not for Jesus I would have chosen death. Jesus saw me through ten births and the deaths of two precious sons. I was almost gone both times, but He brought me back and gave me new friends and new meaning. He put people in place to show me that my life is precious and they will fight along beside me to help me live. My biggest supporter is my husband of twenty-five years.

I think being wealthy is not about money. Being wealthy is about having an ongoing relationship with the living God, and having earthly angels that He puts around you to protect you and see that you come out all right. I thank Him for that.

This book is dedicated to my Mama, to my husband and our amazing family, and also to my Lord Jesus Christ, who is the Savior of my soul.

Conclusion

Why Did Michael Johnston Have to Die?

Emma Johnston is a great-grandmother living a quiet life in a leafy, peaceful backstreet of Durham. Her life is by no means easy. She is overweight and immobile, she contends with a wide array of health issues, she frets at her troubled relationship with her husband, and she struggles to get by on a disability check of $674 a month. Like most of us, she is looking for answers to the problems of life. She wants to be happy, and in spite of all her trials she believes it is possible, so long as she lives one day at a time and remembers to thank God for her daily blessings. She is prey to anxiety and insecurity, but then aren't we all? Emma perhaps has more cause to be anxious than many of us. But then she also has had a lifetime to develop defenses against the misfortunes that life throws at us. She is subject to the same desires as the rest of us. As she trawls the Internet, she regrets that she must turn her back on so many opportunities that she thinks might enrich her life: a Bible study guide, a diet program. But again, Emma has had a lifetime to learn to make do with less. In spite of her poverty, Emma's home is comfortable and safe, even if the surrounding neighborhood is frightening. Emma is able to heat her house in winter. She has satellite TV and broadband Internet. Her husband Jimmy keeps the yard well tended. In this peaceful little house, it is hard to imagine that Emma does not share in the general peace and prosperity of American society.

But of course, Emma has never enjoyed either peace or prosperity for any sustained period. And the poverty and instability that Emma has known for most of her life has extended into the lives of her children and grandchildren.

During the dozens of visits that I paid to Emma's house in order to research this book, I saw the instability and poverty, and their effects, firsthand. I saw Emma desperate because she didn't have a dollar to her name and no food in the pantry to get by for the rest of the month. I saw her children and grandchildren moving into her house because they had nowhere else to go, staying for anything from a week to six months or longer. I saw them eating up Emma's meager supplies, while they struggled with their own problems. I saw Emma too dulled with prescription drugs and hopelessness to even get out of bed. I saw her tend to her pregnant, jobless forty-year-old daughter who had been hit by a car. I saw her fret over her pregnant granddaughter who was going with a drug dealer. I saw her take a call informing her that her daughter was on the run from the police, a suspect in a theft. And I saw her facing the holidays alone in spite of her devotion to her large family.

During her long periods of loneliness and ill health, Emma lives with a heavy burden of memory. Bitterest of all is the memory of her son's murder, which in spite of her faith, Emma cannot put behind her. Michael's death was the reason I met Emma in the first place. It was the reason why we started working together. It is, fundamentally, the reason for this book.

Why did Michael Johnston have to die? Why, in this city of growth and prosperity, in this, the richest, the freest, the most technologically advanced nation on earth, did a young man have to be beaten, kicked and shot five times in a parking lot and then left to die? And why would a killing like that not inspire his community — my community — with outrage? Why would it not bring us out marching in the streets to stop a terrible crime like that from ever happening again? Why would we not close ranks with the family of the deceased? Why, instead, would Michael's death be treated like business as usual, his family ignored and slighted, like outcasts or pariahs?

The answers, in many ways, are as big as America itself. This great democracy, perhaps the noblest political experiment in the history of the human race, has been flawed from the beginning. The Constitution, which initially sanctioned slavery and excluded blacks from participation in the national project, has been patched up to offer a truer vision of equality. But it remains a vision. A constitutional amendment could not quickly alter the structure of American society.

That structure led, even after the abolition of slavery, to a segregated society, in which black citizens were restricted to menial jobs for low pay. Forced off the land by the sharecropping system, rural migrants flooded into the industrial cities in the early decades of the twentieth century in search of jobs. They provided the unskilled labor force for Durham's flourishing tobacco industry. But they were never allowed to participate fully in the city's economic growth. Black families were systematically excluded from skilled and managerial jobs, higher education, high-quality housing, hospital care, access to recreational facilities, and a host of other amenities that defined Durham's growth and success for white families. What went for Durham went also for cities throughout the American South. Durham was known in fact for its relatively progressive atmosphere, an atmosphere that allowed the growth and development of black businesses and the creation of a black middle class. But even the middle class could not overstep certain well-defined limits. A black man, no matter how successful his family, could not go to a white college. He could not eat in a white restaurant. He could not live in a white neighborhood. He could not work as a manager of white employees. And the middle class, for all the justly praised culture and self-respect that it brought to the black community of Durham, was only a small segment of the black population. For the working-class majority, the conditions of life in Durham were little different from those in any other segregated city in America.

It was this social, economic and political structure that created the conditions for Emma's life. It meant that Emma's grandparents were deprived of adequate medical care and died young. It meant that Emma's mother left her rural community without any schooling, in search of economic opportunity. It meant that Emma's father was forced to leave his family because he fell foul of a legal system that was inherently biased against men like him. It meant that Emma would grow up in a society in which nobody expected to go to college or to engage in a professional career, in which dropping out of school was the norm, and in which poverty was the principal fact of life. Did it also explain the culture of violence, abuse, alcoholism and sexual promiscuity that poisoned Emma's childhood? It gets harder to make the connections once the analysis moves to these complex social issues, but it is hard to imagine that a structure of systematic segregation, discrimination, and economic exploitation would not result in some degree of social dysfunction.

These were the legacies that shaped Emma's life. And her life in turn shaped those of her children. The postwar period brought a great alleviation of many of the conditions that worked against the advancement of Durham's black population. The magnificent achievements of the civil rights movement brought integration of the schools, the opening up of skilled and management positions to black men and women, and a positive effort by the city's administration to give a fairer chance to black people. But still, the deeper structural issues remained. Emma's life, like those of the majority of those she grew up with, was characterized by poverty, lack of education, lack of access to skilled jobs, limited health education, constant brushes with the law, a history of violence both inside and outside the family, alcohol and drug abuse, and disintegration of the family structure. On top of that, Emma's children were exposed to the concentration of poverty and social problems in the public housing projects. They were exposed to the new problems of the 1980s forward: in particular, the rapid spread of illegal guns and illegal drugs. Of course Emma's life, and those of her kids, also included plenty of love, warmth, friendship, loyalty, and good times. But for Emma's children, the environment of their upbringing was hardly conducive to the discipline, hard work, academic achievement, and strong family ties that might have helped them to advance into the ranks of the professional middle class.

For a young black male growing up in the housing projects of Durham, the prospects were — and are — exceedingly grim. Society offers few opportunities to a young black man without a high school diploma — and so they drift into the menial jobs of their parents and grandparents, or they hang around on street corners with nothing to do except get into trouble. Once they have any sort of police record, their prospects become dire indeed. It's not surprising that they gravitate toward the gangs, which offer a place to belong, a sense of family, and an income from drugs and other illegal activities that may be many times what they could earn as an hourly wage. These young men become accustomed to being treated as outcasts. They understand that the police are their enemies, not their protectors. Ultimately, they are on their own in a hostile world. And their chances of meeting a violent death are alarmingly high.

As Michael Johnston discovered at the cost of his life, the evil influence of the gangs can extend well beyond their membership. The streets are dangerous for everyone in the gang-infested areas of East Durham. Random shootings are commonplace. And for anyone who gets on the wrong side of a gang member, for whatever reason — a careless word, a look at a girl interpreted the wrong way — the future can be precarious indeed.

The gangs in turn feed on the two greatest evils that afflict our society today: gun violence and the illegal drug trade.

When did our streets become so saturated with guns? It appears that during the 1980s, the safety of our streets took a sharp turn for the worse, as illegal gun use increased dramatically. Safety declined particularly for young black men, who saw disproportional increases in both possession of and injury by illegal guns. Throughout the United States, homicides using guns almost doubled between 1985 and 1995.[1] In Durham, too, the overall homicide rate grew from an average of 16 per year in the second half of the 1980s to 29 per year in the second half of the 1990s.[2] Data on illegal gun ownership is hard to come by, but a 1997 study commissioned by the attorney general found that gun ownership was much more common among people with arrest records than it was among the general population; that arrestees said it was easy and took little time for them to obtain guns illegally; that drug dealers and gang members were more likely even than other arrestees to have such easy access to guns; and, most troublingly, that among juvenile male arrestees, gun ownership and use were much higher than among arrestees generally.[3]

A 1996 Department of Justice report expanded on the results of this disturbing finding. According to the report, from 1985 to 1994 the rate of murder committed nationwide by teens (both black and white) increased by 172 percent. While they constituted only just above one percent of the population, black males aged 14–24 constituted 17 percent of the victims of homicide and over 30 percent of the perpetrators. Since 1984, the number of juveniles killing with a gun had quadrupled, while the number killing with all other weapons combined had remained virtually constant. The largest increase in juvenile homicide involved offenders who were friends and acquaintances of their victims. And from 1989

McDougald Terrace, memorial to a shooting victim. In recent years Durham's housing projects have become stigmatized as "ghettoes" of social dysfunction, violence, and decay. Emma worries that gangs and drug dealers have taken over the streets of McDougald Terrace, where several of her grandchildren are growing up. Forty-five percent of homicides in Durham through the 2000s were classified as gang related (courtesy Terry Shuff).

to 1994, the arrest rate for violent crimes (murder, rape, robbery and aggravated assault) rose over 46 percent among teenagers, but only about 12 percent among adults.[4]

Do any of these trends explain Michael's death? No. The fact remains, and will always remain, that it was senseless and inexplicable. Young men are being shot and killed in our society today for no reason except an infatuation with violence by other young men and boys who are too naive and ill educated to understand the preciousness of a human life. How can we stop them? There will be no easy answers to this deep-rooted problem that continues to take its toll year after year after year. Simply locking up the perpetrators is not going to solve anything. A part

0

of the solution must lie in getting the illegal guns off the streets. A larger part lies in the education system. Our schools are our best chance to influence our kids. Somehow we have to keep them in school, to show them why school is important, to give them a sense of their own value as productive members of society, and to show them the infinite possibility that is open to a young man or woman with education in this country.

The Other Side of Durham's Growth and Prosperity

Michael's death was the worst thing that has happened in Emma's life. But it is also just one among a train of disasters that has afflicted her throughout her life. Emma and her immediate family members have been the victims of child abuse and rape, domestic violence and beatings, gun violence and murder, alcoholism and drug addiction, ill health and disability, fatal accidents and police negligence, poverty and discrimination, and a host of lesser ills, injustices, grievances and misfortunes. As I worked with Emma on this history, I was constantly struck by the contrast between Emma's story and the standard narratives of Durham's postwar history, and, by extension, those of other growing cities in America's "New South."

There have been more than a dozen books published on Durham's history, and hundreds more on other cities around the South, and on southern history in general. For the most part these seem to fit into two alternative narrative patterns.

On one hand, there is the "white" story of economic growth and cultural development. Most of the published histories of Durham fall into this category.[5] They emphasize the achievements of the city's business and political leaders (mostly white), and they paint a rosy picture of a society that has come a long way from its origins as a railway depot with just a handful of residents.

On the other hand, there is the "black" narrative.[6] Several of these memorialize the vibrant black community of Durham in the first half of the twentieth century—a community which W.E.B. DuBois called a "city of cities to look for the prosperity of Negroes."[7] But in lauding the progress of the black middle class, this narrative tends to ignore the plight of the thousands of working-class black residents who benefited little from this prosperity. For example, much of the property in Hayti was owned by W.G. Pearson, a black educator and cofounder of the Farmers and Merchants Bank. Pearson was the biggest slum lord in Durham, and for all his achievements, his tenants can hardly be seen as having benefited from the fact that he was black and middle class.

The postwar histories of African Americans in the South focus overwhelmingly on the civil rights movement and the enormous gains made by blacks as a result of its successes. These are powerful and moving stories. The civil rights activists in Durham struggled against great odds, in the face of implacable hostility and even violence. They faced a system that was systematically weighted against them, so that even as they fought using the tools of a civilized society — the law courts, peaceful demonstrations, and sit-ins — those same tools were manipulated in a constant effort to undermine and destroy them. And they prevailed. The immediate goals of civil rights activism were essentially met by the end of the 1960s, and since then Durham has made enormous strides in opening up its political, administrative, and economic institutions to black citizens. Today, color is no longer a bar to access to the city's elected positions.

And yet, a striking feature of the stories of civil rights battles and their eventual victories is the middle-class origins of most of the activists. Floyd McKissick, for example, was the first African American student to be admitted to the University of North Carolina law school. He came from a middle-class family in Asheville. He went on to become a prominent black lawyer in Durham and a leader of the Congress of Racial Equality. His two daughters were the first black students to enroll in the all-white Durham High School. Nathan Garrett was the son of a pharmacist, not wealthy but solidly middle class. He attended Yale University and became a CPA in Durham and one of the leaders in the struggle for black economic progress. Indeed, the political and cultural life of Durham today is enriched by a sparkling group of alumni of the struggle for civil rights and racial equality — almost all of whom emerged from Durham's flourishing black middle class.

These are stirring stories. But they seem to have little bearing on the life and experiences of Emma Johnston or her children. Indeed, the overwhelming impression that Emma's story has left on me is that there is a third, generally untold narrative of Durham's history. It is a narrative that has a startlingly different shape from the story of white-led growth and prosperity, or the story of black-led civil rights and equality. The trajectory in almost every published account of Durham's history is sharply upward. Yes, there may be nostalgia for Durham's past traditions and communities, but the Durham of today is incomparably better than the Durham of sixty years ago. It offers far more economic opportunity. It has a far richer cultural life. It offers far more equal rights to blacks and minorities. It is diverse, friendly, and fun yet affordable. One can literally visualize the upward curve of these stories as injustices are fought and conquered, opportunities expanded, communities deepened and enriched, and growth assured as an essential element of Durham's community life.

Where does Emma's story fit in these upward trajectories? What strikes me most forcibly about Emma's story is how little has changed for her or her family — how *flat* her life story has been.

Emma was born into poverty. She has been poor her entire life. And today she is as poor as ever.

Emma's children are poor. One or two of them have been able to achieve a measure of financial stability, but only one of them owns her own home; many of them depend on welfare checks to get by from month to month; and some of them appear to be on the brink of homelessness.

And Emma's grandchildren are poor too. Many of them have gone through the foster care system, and they have emerged on the other side with little ability to make their own way in the world. Several have experienced actual homelessness. Several also appear to be experiencing the same problems that afflicted Emma during her own youth: teenage pregnancy, domestic violence, brushes with the law, and drug and alcohol abuse.

Emma grew up in a segregated society, she lived her whole life in effective segregation, and she lives today in a world in which black and white remain apart. This was to me one of the most intriguing contrasts with the more traditional narrative of postwar Durham's history. What happened to the gains of the civil rights movement? What happened to the struggle for integration? Certainly, Emma would have the right today to sit in the front of a bus, or to eat in a white-owned restaurant. But her daily reality is one of a black society, in which her only contacts with the white world are either administrative — visits to the doctor, for example — or, as in my own relationship with her, the indirect result of her son's tragic death. And Emma's friends consider her to have an unusual number of contacts with the white community!

Emma's children and grandchildren attended schools that were theoretically integrated. But as a result of white flight to the suburbs and the continued concentration of the black community in low-income neighborhoods, the schools they attended were almost entirely black — with a slowly growing Latino component in the case of the younger children and grandchildren. Burton Elementary School, which most of Emma's children attended, in 2010 had only 9 white students out of a school population of 358.[8] Moreover, the mostly black and Latino inner-city schools have performed poorly on standardized tests compared to city, state, and national averages. To take one example, at Burton Elementary in 2007–8, only 29 percent of third graders were at grade level in math end-of-year tests, and only 19 percent were at grade level for reading.[9] Whether the schools have failed the students, or whether the students' disadvantaged family environments are to blame, is an open question.

And the neighborhoods in which Emma has lived have also been almost entirely black as well as low-income. In 2008, 94 percent of the families supported by the Durham Housing Authority through traditional public housing or through the Section 8 program were black.[10] In theory, Section 8 households (who receive rent vouchers from the federal government) are free to live in any neighborhood they choose, but in practice most stay close to the neighborhoods they know. Emma's Section 8 house is just a few blocks away from McDougald Terrace, where she lived for much of her adult life. All of the residents in Emma's street are black. For Emma, this does not seem like discrimination. It just seems a matter of course. But there are consequences to living in a low-income black neighborhood. None of the grocery store chains has a branch in the area. The nearest bank branch is more than three miles away, in Northgate Mall. Many services appear to cost more for the residents of Emma's neighborhood than they would for citizens living in more affluent parts of Durham. Durham may be garnering praise for its diversity, but there is nothing diverse about Emma's neighborhood. The same applies to her children and grandchildren, all of whom live in overwhelmingly black neighborhoods.

In short, Emma and her family have failed to participate in virtually any of the upward trajectories of Durham's postwar history. They have not benefited from job growth; they were not involved in the civil rights movement, nor have they particularly benefited from it; they have not participated in the opportunities in higher education; they have not benefited from the growing knowledge and IT industries — although growth in Duke University, particularly the medical facilities, has at times offered them menial job opportunities; they have not shared in the growing diversity; and they have not been able to take advantage of cultural growth in the arts, music, or food culture.

That said, there are some areas where Emma and her family have clearly benefited from the postwar transformation of American society. Most notably, they have benefited from the expanded welfare system, which has provided most members of Emma's family with both monetary and medical benefits. Emma has been on some form of welfare for much of her life — more when she was on her own, less (or none) when she was being supported by a husband. Welfare — including housing benefits — has provided her with a roof over her head ever since she moved into her first apartment at the turn of the 1970s. It has provided her with child-support payments that enabled her to feed and clothe her children. It has provided her with food subsidies. And in more recent years it has provided her with Supplemental Security Income disability benefits. Thanks to welfare, in addition to the support of some of the men in her life, Emma has been able to live her entire life and raise six children without ever having to go out to work. Whether or not this was the intention of the welfare system, for Emma it has been an unquestionable benefit. For all her hardships in other areas, Emma's material life has been easy compared with, for example, that of her mother, who had to work long shifts in a hot, smelly, dusty tobacco factory from the age of thirteen.

Even more beneficial has been Emma's access to medical care. Throughout their lives, the Medicaid program has provided Emma and most of her children with free access to good-quality health services — services that would have cost them hundreds of thousands of dollars in the private system. Unfortunately, Emma herself and several of her family members have been intensive users of the system. Emma has suffered from a variety of increasingly serious ailments since she was in her mid-thirties. The medical system provides her with a complex array of services, including doctor's visits, MRI scans, clinical tests, prescription drug deliveries, emergency services, and hospitalization.

Some of Emma's children appear to be even more intensive users of the system, combining a range of physical ailments with mental health problems requiring drug intervention and close monitoring by health providers. Emma and her family members suffer at times from the inefficiency and apparent carelessness of parts of the system — for example, mental health services have recently been outsourced to a third-party provider, causing disruptions in continuity and less personal treatment — but overall the quality of services seems to have risen over the years along with the development of Durham's health system overall and with the increase in ailments suffered by family members. Given the seriousness of Emma's medical condition, it seems entirely reasonable to assume that without this assistance, she would by now be dead.

Black and Poor in Postwar America

Emma's story is her own, and it cannot be taken as representative of any particular group or community. But there is no doubt that the circumstances that shaped Emma's life also shaped those of millions of other poor black families across America.

For more than twenty years, Emma lived in public housing projects in Durham. In this experience, she was a part of a vast experiment that took place on a national scale. Indeed, the entire program of public housing was bankrolled by the federal government as part of a program intended to revive America's inner-city areas and eliminate the evils of private "slum" dwellings. Over time, the housing projects have come to be stereotyped as a massive failure. "The projects" have become a byword for grim concrete towers filled with violence, dirt and despair. Of course, the reality of public housing has been far more complex than that. Many of the experiments in public housing that have garnered the most praise or criticism have been huge developments in inner-city areas — New York, Chicago, and St. Louis, for example. Among these, experiences have diverged widely. New York's public housing is generally considered quite successful. The vast system houses almost half a million people. There are long waiting lists to get into many of New York's housing projects, and the residents are very diverse in their backgrounds and family circumstances. Former residents of the New York public housing projects include Lloyd Blankfein, chairman and CEO of Goldman Sachs, and Supreme Court justice Sonia Sotomayor.[11] By contrast, projects in Chicago and St. Louis have been much less successful. The notorious Pruitt-Igoe project in St. Louis, a complex of thirty-three high-rise buildings which was demolished only sixteen years after its completion, became a symbol of the failures of public housing.

Durham's housing projects are in contrast to all of these big-city developments. McDougald Terrace, where Emma lived, is on a much more human scale. Its 360 two-storey units are spacious, well built, in small blocks, and surrounded by leafy suburban streets. Clearly, Durham did not suffer from the ills of misguided architectural modernism that is sometimes attributed as one of the causes of failure. Indeed, probably few would argue that Durham's public housing has failed. As in much of the nation, public housing remains a vital part of the overall housing mix in Durham. It caters not only to the long-term poor, but also to immigrant and elderly families, and many others with special needs.

However, one effect of the Durham public housing program, like many others throughout the United States, has been to concentrate poor minority families in distinct geographic areas, which have then become stigmatized as "ghettoes" of social dysfunction, violence, and decay. The public housing projects were not originally intended as welfare projects. They were for working-class families, people like Emma's mother who had steady jobs but, in the view of the planners, needed help moving up from their "slum" accommodation (which Emma remembers as being far from slumlike) to a higher standard of housing. But the fact is that the

McDougald project was explicitly built for black tenants. And over time, further economic marginalization of its residents led to the "extreme racial, economic and social isolation"[12] that characterized the public housing experience across much of America.

These problems have been exacerbated by the funding problems of housing authorities throughout the United States. Ironically, with federal subsidies in place, raising the money to build a public housing project was much easier than raising funds to maintain it. Citizens tend to resent local taxes and keep a sharp eye out for expenses they deem unnecessary. Public housing funding was often denied, in part because of a perception that if the residents were going to vandalize their own dwellings, then they did not deserve to have them repaired. There can be no doubt that vandalism was high in the Durham public housing system, as it was around America. Some studies attribute this to the extremely young demographic of many projects.[13] But the problem was made much worse by the difficulties in finding funds to maintain the projects to an acceptable standard.

Emma's life has also been shaped by the problems of illegal drugs, crime, and violence, including gang violence. All of these have been major national issues in recent years, and there are surely many areas in which the experiences of Emma and her family reflect national trends.

Gangs and violence have played a key role in the issues of race and poverty that haunt cities across the United States. They are in turn linked to the problems of public housing, which is said to have "provided gangs with cohesion because it was an identifiable and secure home base."[14] The gangs have been on the periphery of Emma's life. None of her children have been directly involved in them, and only one grandchild seems to be at risk. But the influence of the gangs reaches far beyond their membership. Emma's son Michael got on the wrong side of some gang members and paid for it with his life. Emma also worries about the safety of all her grandchildren, particularly her granddaughter Bethany. While this book was being written, Bethany became pregnant by a man Emma suspected of being a drug pusher and a gang member. Bethany delivered the baby, but it was stillborn. Soon after, Bethany herself was arrested for drug dealing and incarcerated in the Durham County jail for several weeks.

Gang problems developed in Durham somewhat later than in the big cities, but as in the rest of America, gangs have become an explosive issue in the past decade. As demand for illegal drugs expanded in small cities and suburban areas in the 1990s, the gangs followed to meet the demand. If there were existing smaller gangs in operation, violent turf wars often followed. According to the FBI, gang activity in the Southeast has expanded from 49 percent of communities in 2004 to 68 percent in 2008. Similarly, the number of students nationwide reporting gang activity in their schools increased from 29 percent to 36 percent in urban schools, and from 18 percent to 21 percent in suburban schools, between 2001 and 2005.[15] Nationally, at least one million gang members were reported throughout the United States (147,000 of them in jail) in 2008, up from 800,000 in 2005.

The city of Durham produced its own gang assessment report in 2007. The Durham police department began attempting to measure gang membership and gang activity in 2002. Estimates from that year put gang membership at only one hundred, increasing to two hundred in 2003, four hundred in 2004, and one thousand by 2007, with another two thousand youths being considered at serious risk of being drawn into gang membership. Twenty-five percent of gang members were eighteen or younger, while 30 percent were nineteen to twenty-one years old. However, nearly one-third of *arrested* gang members were seventeen years old or younger, and half were nineteen or younger. According to police data, there were fifty documented gang members sixteen or younger in Durham in 2006. Eighty-two percent of documented gang members, and 93 percent of those arrested in 2006, were African American. On average, 45 percent of homicides in Durham through the 2000s were classified as gang related.[16]

Gun violence was present in Emma's life from her childhood. Her mother was shot not by a gang member but by a drunken friend. Her husband turned out to have an armory of illegal guns under Emma's house. Emma's friend was shot by a jealous ex-boyfriend. And the entire community, including the victim, seemed to take this as a matter of course. More recently, the spread of illegal guns and their easy availability has surely contributed to the rising toll of gun violence among African American men. The factors that made it so easy for a group of ill-educated and thoughtless young men to obtain the guns to shoot Michael Johnston have also contributed to the epidemic of gun violence afflicting young black men across the nation.

In Emma's own recollection, illegal drugs have been the most baneful influence of all on the fortunes of her family. Certainly, illegal drug use is a major national problem that contributes to family dysfunction and that feeds the epidemic of gangs and violence. But it is important also not to stereotype the nation's experience based on anecdotes about one or a few families. This is particularly true since myths about crack cocaine use have been used to stigmatize entire segments of the population — particularly poor black women, the very segment to which Emma and her daughters belong.

It is hard to say how typical Emma's family's experiences have been. Drug use is certainly widespread in the United States, but it crosses all class, age, race, and gender boundaries. Marijuana in particular is very widespread, with 28 percent of young adults reporting using it in any given year between 2004 and 2008, and roughly 13 percent of adolescents. Cocaine use is also widespread, with around 6 percent of young adults and 1.5 percent of adolescents using it each year. Crack cocaine, the drug specified by Emma as the greatest threat to her children, is relatively little used, with less than one percent of adults or adolescents using it in a given year. In fact, the other major category of illegal drug use is prescription narcotics, which 12 percent of young adults reported using.[17] In this area, Emma herself may be as great a drug user as her children — although her sources are perfectly legal.

Given its relatively low profile in the overall picture of drug use, it is surprising how much attention crack cocaine has received. During the 1980s in particular, images of crack-addicted mothers and damaged "crackbaby" fetuses were widespread in the media. The images almost always portrayed black women, and they were often used in the context of discussions on welfare reform. The implication was that irresponsible black women were exploiting the welfare system to purchase crack and then producing children who would be a permanent burden on American society.[18] Emma does not suggest that her grandchildren were affected by in utero crack use, but her portraits of her own daughters abusing crack and alcohol at the expense of their children do seem to reinforce these stereotypes.

Accompanying the stereotype of the crack mother was that of the "welfare mother," a typified woman, usually portrayed as black, who was reputed to have babies just so that she could claim additional welfare checks under the Aid to Families with Dependent Children program. Studies showed that by the mid–1970s, many people had come to automatically associate welfare with African American women, even though the actual recipients of welfare were much more diverse.[19]

These stereotypes in turn fed into the debate over welfare reform. Among other things the reform movement took aim at the AFDC fund, which was accused of encouraging welfare mothers to breed indiscriminately in the knowledge that the more children they had the more welfare they would get — thus, by implication, further perpetuating the cycle of poverty. As one influential columnist wrote, "A family that works does not get a raise for having a child. Why then should a family that doesn't work?"[20] This is in fact untrue: working families get significant tax breaks for each additional child. But more pertinent is the fact that family sizes of welfare recipients were actually smaller than the population as a whole: 2.9 persons in 1992, compared to 3.2 persons for all American families. In 1993, New Jersey actually acted on the perception that women were abusing the system by having more babies, prohibiting the payment of additional ADFC benefits to women who conceived while on welfare. The measure does appear to have increased the abortion rate among welfare recipients, but over the longer term, family size among welfare recipients in New Jersey did not decline as a result of the measure.[21]

After the welfare reform of 1996, millions of recipients were taken off the welfare rolls, giving rise to increasing concerns about the vulnerability of America's poorest families, including children. The measure reduced America's welfare rolls by more than half, from 4.4 million to 2.1 million by 2001. The idea was that welfare recipients were to be trained and helped into the workforce, where they would be able to pull themselves out of poverty and dependency. The reality, though, was that millions of single mothers were forced into minimum-wage jobs, forcing them to make ad hoc arrangements for the care of their children and doing nothing to raise them out of poverty. As one commentator stated, "They get by in the same way the poor of New Orleans and Haiti are getting by, by cobbling together every available source of aid and support, and then trying to learn how to adjust to constant suffering and insecurity. Increasing rates of domestic violence are just one hidden story here."[22]

With regard to welfare, Emma's family story is mixed and does not seem to reflect any particular national trend or experience. Emma herself had many children and claimed welfare benefits for most of them. But to characterize Emma as a "welfare mother" who deliberately had children to increase her income would be a gross distortion. Emma's family background was Catholic. She strongly disapproved of abortion, for herself or for her children — even when they were pregnant as young teenagers. More importantly, Emma always saw her children as a deeply positive element in her life. Even her first child, born when Emma was far too young and ill prepared, brought forth all of the instinctive love and joy that any mother would feel. Emma's love for her children has been an abiding strength in her life, and it would be unimaginable to attribute her child bearing to some sort of economic calculation. Similarly, Emma's children did not benefit significantly from the welfare system as a result of having children. Both Anna and Brianna signed their children away into the foster care system, while Emma's other children did not have many children of their own.

On the other hand, Emma and her family seem to have come through the welfare reform of 1996 without any significant alteration of their benefits. In Emma's case, by the mid–1990s her child benefits had been replaced by disability payments, which made her exempt from the reform program's work requirements. Three of her children are also receiving disability. Emma and several of her children receive food stamps, but those too were unaffected by the reform.

What about some of the more positive aspects of the postwar experiences of poor black women? How has Emma's life reflected those?

Throughout the United States, poor black women were not just passive recipients of welfare aid, herded into the projects. Rather, many of them played an active role in the struggle to improve their lot, in spite of severe disadvantages. In *Our Separate Ways*, Christina Greene describes the heroic struggles of activist women in postwar Durham, many of them from similar backgrounds to Emma.[23] Such struggles were visible across the country. In the Pruitt-Igoe projects, where able-bodied men were expressly forbidden from living, women were involved in every aspect of the community's economic and social life, often in the face of overwhelming obstacles.[24] One of the common features of many of these women's experiences is the absence of men able to play an active role in their lives. Women were forced to take control of difficult circumstances, including taking care of grandchildren; fighting for better treatment at the hands of social services, housing authority, and the men in their own community; and dealing with health and behavior problems within their own families.

This positive agency of women in their own lives and destinies certainly mirrors Emma's experience. Emma has been a powerful force in her family and in her community, fighting for the rights of her children and grandchildren, supporting them when they were in trouble, and taking on the city authorities including the police as she fought against perceived injustices. Emma took a strong interest in her community, doing faithful duty as vice president of the McDougald Terrace Tenants Steering Committee, and in many other ways she has shown herself to be one of a line of strong women who have been the backbone of their community for generations.

Emma's experiences, then, reflect some of the key issues of race, class, and gender that have been so central to America's postwar history, but they are by no means stereotypical. In fact, her story helps us to be aware of how careful we should be about stereotyping any one group. To me, what shines through most strongly from Emma's story, and what cannot easily be measured in any national study or survey, is the love and dedication that has characterized so much of her life. No matter what trouble she herself has been in, no matter what mistakes her children have made, Emma has been there for them. Her society may have been abusive and at times dysfunctional, but the love that Emma gave to and received from her children and grandchildren, husbands, boy-friends, drinking partners, and childhood friends was real and lasting. In spite of betrayal and abuse, Emma has remained loyal to those she loved. Many of them have been friends since their childhood almost sixty years ago. The loyalty and connection, the comfort and closeness that Emma feels for her community is in paradoxical contrast to the social dysfunction, fragmentation, and transience of so many elements of her society.

And in spite of all Emma's hardships, it is enviable. How many of us can say that we still keep up with our friends from elementary school? How many of us have friends with whom we have regularly met and laughed for the last fifty years? How many of us can depend on that kind of support network—a network that has, in the end, seen Emma through a lifetime of hardship and trials?

In the end, Emma's story is not the story of America, or even of a segment of American society. It is the story of Emma—a unique individual with many extraordinary qualities. As I have worked on this project with her, I have been struck again and again at her articulacy, at her lively humor and wit, at her amazing storytelling ability, at her spiritual depth, and at her wisdom. I have learned so much from Emma Johnston, about a life that has been as full and committed as that of any man or woman I have known. I have learned about strength in the face of adversity. I have learned about dignity in the face of discrimination and denied opportunity. And often, I have wondered. Emma Johnston is a woman of enormous talent and personality. What if our positions had been reversed? What if she had grown up with all the privileges of a member of the white middle class? What wonderful things might she have been able to accomplish? And what if I had grown up poor and disadvantaged? Would I have made of my life even a fraction of what she has achieved?

Chapter Notes

Introduction

1. http://www.durhampolice.com/news/pdf/071220_1.pdf, p. 40.
2. http://www.durham-nc.com/bullseye/archive/vol6_09.pdf.
3. Durham Youth Coordinating Board, *The State of Durham's Children 2000* (Durham, NC: The Board, 2000).
4. Custom table from http://factfinder.census.gov.

Chapter 1

1. Quoted in Christina Greene, *Our Separate Ways: Women and the Black Freedom Movement in Durham, North Carolina* (Chapel Hill: University of North Carolina Press, 2005), 12.
2. *Ibid.*
3. William Towe, *Barriers to Black Political Participation in North Carolina* (Atlanta: Voter Education Project, 1972), 7.
4. *Ibid.*, 10.
5. City of Durham, *Durham City Code,* 1947 (Durham, NC: City of Durham, 1972), 142.
6. Edith Wilkinson, *Pattern of Negro Segregation in Durham, North Carolina* (PhD diss., Duke University, 1950), 127.
7. Paul Finkelman, ed., *Encyclopedia of African American History, 1896 to the Present: From the Age of Segregation to the Twenty-First Century* (New York: Oxford University Press, 2009), 3:27.
8. Edith Wilkinson, *Pattern of Negro Segregation in Durham, North Carolina* (PhD diss., Duke University, 1950), 26–27.
9. *Ibid.*, 41–43.
10. *Ibid.*, 48–51.
11. *Ibid.*, 100–101.

12. *Ibid.*, chap. 1.
13. Leslie Brown, *Upbuilding Black Durham: Gender, Class, and Black Community Development in the Jim Crow South* (Chapel Hill: University of North Carolina Press, 2008), 229.
14. Hugh Brinton, *The Negro in Durham: A Study of Adjustment to Town Life* (PhD diss., UNC Chapel Hill, 1930), 115. The entire description is from Brinton, 107–131.
15. *Ibid.*, 129.
16. *Ibid.*, 117.
17. *Ibid.*, 118.
18. *Ibid.*, 122.
19. Leslie Brown, *Upbuilding Black Durham: Gender, Class, and Black Community Development in the Jim Crow South* (Chapel Hill: University of North Carolina Press, 2008), 228.
20. *Ibid.*
21. Christina Greene, *Our Separate Ways: Women and the Black Freedom Movement in Durham, North Carolina* (Chapel Hill: University of North Carolina Press, 2005), 29.
22. Leslie Brown, *Upbuilding Black Durham: Gender, Class, and Black Community Development in the Jim Crow South* (Chapel Hill: University of North Carolina Press, 2008), 166.
23. *Ibid.*, 182.
24. Edith Wilkinson, *Pattern of Negro Segregation in Durham, North Carolina* (PhD diss., Duke University, 1950), 17.
25. John Picott, *A Survey of the Public Schools of Durham, North Carolina* (Durham, NC: n.p., 1950), 15.
26. *Ibid.*, 46.
27. *Ibid.*, 86.
28. *Ibid.*, 73.

Chapter 2

1. *Durham Herald,* July 6, 1958.
2. Operation Breakthrough, *A Profile of Community Problems: Durham County* (Raleigh, NC: North Carolina Fund, 1964).
3. For this section I am indebted to the following sources: June Axinn, *Social Welfare: A History of the American Response to Need* (Boston: Pearson/Allyn and Bacon, 2005), 243–254; Walter Trattner, *From Poor Law to Welfare State: A History of Social Welfare in America* (New York: Free Press, 1999), 288–300; U.S. Department of Health and Human Services, "A Brief History of the AFDC Program," http://aspe.hhs.gov/ hsp/AFDC/baseline/1history.pdf.
4. Census Data, 1970 (provided through Social Explorer, www.socialexplorer.com); North Carolina Fund, *Characteristics of Individuals in Areas Served by the Community Action Program in the City of Durham* (Durham: North Carolina Fund, 1967).
5. Jean Anderson, *Durham County* (Durham, NC: Duke University Press, 1999), 412–13.

Chapter 3

1. Jean Anderson, *Durham County* (Durham, NC: Duke University Press, 1999), 411.
2. *Ibid.,* 409.
3. *Ibid.,* 477.

Chapter 4

1. Ronald Brown, *An Analysis of the Incidence of Crime with Selected Socio-Economic Variables in Durham, North Carolina* (Durham, NC: Durham Urban Observatory, 1976), 7–20.
2. Jack McElreath, *The Cost of Opportunity: School Desegregation and Changing Race Relations in the Triangle since World War II* (PhD diss., University of Pennsylvania, 2002), 387.

Chapter 5

1. http://www.dcvb-nc.com/cr/Durham_Accolades.pdf.
2. *Herald-Sun,* December 10, 2006.

3. http://www.durham-nc.com/bulls eye/archive/vol6_09.pdf.
4. http://www.durhampolice.com/news/ pdf/090904_1.pdf.
5. Durham Youth Coordinating Board, *The State of Durham's Children 2000* (Durham, NC: The Board, 2000).
6. http://www.kff.org/minorityhealth/ upload/7541.pdf.

Conclusion

1. http://www.nij.gov/topics/crime/gu n-violence.
2. US Department of Justice Uniform Crime Reporting Statistics (online tool, http://www.ucrdatatool.gov/index.cfm).
3. http://www.ncjrs.gov/pdffiles/16349 6.pdf.
4. http://bjs.ojp.usdoj.gov/content/pub/ pdf/tjvfox2.pdf.
5. See, for instance, Johnston Wise, *Durham: A Bull City Story* (Charleston, SC: Arcadia, 2002); Mena Webb, *The Way We Were: Remembering Durham* (Durham, NC: Historic Preservation Society of Durham, 2003); Johnston Wise, *Durham County* (Charleston, SC: Arcadia, 2000); Joel Kostyu, *Durham, a Pictorial History* (Norfolk, VA: Donning, 1978); Johnston Wise, *Durham Tales: the Morris Street Maple, the Plastic Cow, the Durham Day That Was & More* (Charleston, SC: History Press, 2008). One excellent work that encompasses both "black" and "white" narratives is Jean Anderson, *Durham County* (Durham, NC: Duke University Press, 1999).
6. See, for example, Dorothy Phelps Jones, *The End of an Era* (Durham, NC: Brown Enterprises, 2001); Andre Vann, *Durham's Hayti* (Charleston, SC: Arcadia, 1999); Leslie Brown, *Upbuilding Black Durham: Gender, Class, and Black Community Development in the Jim Crow South* (Chapel Hill: University of North Carolina Press, 2008); Chris Howard, *Keep Your Eyes on the Prize: The Black Struggle for Civic Equality in Durham, North Carolina, 1954– 1963* (PhD diss., Duke University, 1983); Christina Greene, *Our Separate Ways: Women and the Black Freedom Movement in Durham, North Carolina* (Chapel Hill: University of North Carolina Press, 2005).

7. http://maghis.oxfordjournals.org/content/18/2/23.extract.

8. http://www.dpsnc.net/images/pdf/enrollment/ADM_2010.11.pdf.

9. http://www.dpsnc.net/about-dps/district-stats-and-scores/scores/elementary-eog/burton-geo-world-magnet. The performance increased substantially in the following years.

10. http://www.durhamnc.gov/Departments/ComDev/pdf/market_needs_analysis030611.pdf, p. 4.

11. http://en.wikipedia.org/wiki/New_York_City_Housing_Authority.

12. Bradford Hunt, *Blueprint for Disaster: The Unraveling of Chicago Public Housing* (Chicago: Chicago University Press, 2009), 286.

13. *Ibid.*, 12.

14. Daniel J. Monti, "Gangs in More-and Less-Settled Communities," in Scott Cummins and Daniel J. Monti (eds.), *Gangs: The Origins and Impact of Contemporary Youth Gangs in the United States* (Albany, NY: State University of New York Press, 1993), 219–253.

15. http://www.justice.gov/ndic/pubs32/32146/gangs.htm#start.

16. http://www.durhampolice.com/news/pdf/071220_1.pdf.

17. http://www.justice.gov/ndic/pubs38/38661/app-b.htm#Top.

18. See Eve Mahan, *Crack Cocaine, Crime, and Women: Legal, Social, and Treatment Issues* (Thousand Oaks, CA: Sage, 1996); Drew Humphries, *Crack Mothers: Pregnancy, Drugs, and the Media* (Columbus: Ohio State University Press, 1999).

19. http://en.wikipedia.org/wiki/Welfare_queen.

20. *Boston Globe*, April 16, 1992.

21. http://www.welfareacademy.org/pubseval/crs.shtml. See also Howard Gensler, ed., *The American Welfare System: Origins, Structure, and Effects* (Westport, CT: Praeger, 1996).

22. http://www.thenation.com/article/what-ever-happened-welfare-mothers. The commentator is Sharon Hayes, author of *Flat Broke with Children: Women in the Age of Welfare Reform* (New York: Oxford University Press, 2003).

23. Christina Greene, *Our Separate Ways: Women and the Black Freedom Movement in Durham, North Carolina* (Chapel Hill: University of North Carolina Press, 2005).

24. Lee Rainwater, *Behind Ghetto Walls: Black Families in a Federal Slum* (New Brunswick, NJ: Transaction Publishers, 2006). See also the documentary film *The Pruitt-Igie Myth* (2011).

Bibliography

Anderson, Jean. *Durham County* (Durham, NC: Duke University Press, 1999).

Axinn, June. *Social Welfare: A History of the American Response to Need* (Boston: Pearson/Allyn and Bacon, 2005).

Brinton, Hugh. *The Negro in Durham: A Study of Adjustment to Town Life* (PhD diss., UNC Chapel Hill, 1930).

Brown, Leslie. *Upbuilding Black Durham: Gender, Class, and Black Community Development in the Jim Crow South* (Chapel Hill: University of North Carolina Press, 2008).

Brown, Ronald. *An Analysis of the Incidence of Crime with Selected Socio-Economic Variables in Durham, North Carolina* (Durham, NC: Durham Urban Observatory, 1976).

City of Durham. *Durham City Code, 1947* (Durham, NC: City of Durham, 1972).

Cummins, Scott, and Daniel J. Monti, eds. *Gangs: The Origins and Impact of Contemporary Youth Gangs in the United States* (Albany: State University of New York Press, 1993).

Durham Youth Coordinating Board. *The State of Durham's Children 2000* (Durham, NC: Durham Youth Coordinating Board, 2000).

Finkelman, Paul, ed. *Encyclopedia of African American History, 1896 to the Present: From the Age of Segregation to the Twenty-First Century* (New York: Oxford University Press, 2009), vol. 3.

Gensler, Howard, ed. *The American Welfare System: Origins, Structure, and Effects* (Westport: Praeger, 1996).

Greene, Christina. *Our Separate Ways: Women and the Black Freedom Movement in Durham, North Carolina* (Chapel Hill: University of North Carolina Press, 2005).

Hayes, Sharon. *Flat Broke with Children: Women in the Age of Welfare Reform* (New York: Oxford University Press, 2003).

Howard, Chris. *Keep Your Eyes on the Prize: The Black Struggle for Civic Equality in Durham, North Carolina, 1954–1963* (PhD diss., Duke University, 1983).

Humphries, Drew. *Crack Mothers: Pregnancy, Drugs, and the Media* (Columbus: Ohio State University Press, 1999).

Hunt, Bradford. *Blueprint for Disaster: The Unraveling of Chicago Public Housing* (Chicago: Chicago University Press, 2009).

Jones, Dorothy Phelps. *The End of an Era* (Durham, NC: Brown Enterprises, 2001).

Kostyu, Joel. *Durham, a Pictorial History* (Norfolk: Donning, 1978).

Mahan, Eve. *Crack Cocaine, Crime, and Women: Legal, Social, and Treatment Issues* (Thousand Oaks, CA: Sage, 1996).

McElreath, Jack. *The Cost of Opportunity: School Desegregation and Changing Race Relations in the Triangle since World War II* (PhD diss., University of Pennsylvania, 2002).

North Carolina Fund. *Characteristics of Individuals in Areas Served by the Community Action Program in the City of Durham* (Durham: North Carolina Fund, 1967).

Operation Breakthrough. *A Profile of*

Community Problems: Durham County (Raleigh: North Carolina Fund, 1964).

Picott, John. *A Survey of the Public Schools of Durham, North Carolina* (Durham, NC: n.p., 1950).

Rainwater, Lee. *Behind Ghetto Walls: Black Families in a Federal Slum* (New Brunswick: Transaction Publishers, 2006).

Towe, William. *Barriers to Black Political Participation in North Carolina* (Atlanta: Voter Education Project, 1972).

Trattner, Walter. *From Poor Law to Welfare State: A History of Social Welfare in America* (New York: Free Press, 1999).

Vann, Andre. *Durham's Hayti* (Charleston, SC: Arcadia, 1999).

Webb, Mena. *The Way We Were: Remembering Durham* (Durham, NC: Historic Preservation Society of Durham, 2003).

Wilkinson, Edith. *Pattern of Negro Segregation in Durham, North Carolina* (PhD diss., Duke University, 1950).

Wise, Johnston. *Durham: A Bull City Story* (Charleston, SC: Arcadia, 2002).

_____. *Durham County* (Charleston, SC: Arcadia, 2000).

_____. *Durham Tales: The Morris Street Maple, the Plastic Cow, the Durham Day That Was & More* (Charleston, SC: History Press, 2008).

Index